GW00602718

Straightforward Guides

WRITING YOUR OWN LIFE STORY

Nicholas Corder

Straightforward Publishing
www.straightforwardco.co.uk

Straightforward Guides
Brighton BN1 6AA

British-cataloguing-in-Publication-Data. A catalogue record for this book
is available from the British Library.

ISBN 184716 022 0
ISBN 13: 978184716 022 5

Printed by Biddles Ltd Kings Lynn Norfolk

Cover design by Bookworks Islington

Acknowledgements

With many thanks to all my creative writing students, from whom I have learned far more than they ever have from me. I would also like to give special thanks to the following who have agreed to have excerpts of their work in this book:

Rita Bell
Jim Billsborough
Norma Brannan
Pat Graham
Heather Graves
Audrey Paley
Evelyn Rutherford
Susan Stokes
Cath Sweeney
Maureen Toyn
Flo Wightman

This book is dedicated to my wife Pauline whose constant cries of "Get back in there and write, you idle fool!" are the reason I managed to finish this book.

Contents

Writing Your Own Life Story

....

Introduction

"There is properly no history; only biography." Ralph Waldo Emerson

Summer 1919. A troop carrier pulls away from its temporary mooring in Newcastle-upon-Tyne. It is carrying soldiers under the command of General Ironside, destined for the White Sea port of Archangel. Here, they will fight in support of the White Russians, the Tsarist force that is attempting to wrest control of Russia from its new communist leaders.

Amongst the men on board, is Sergeant Frederick Corder of the Royal Engineers, an exiled Londoner. He is being paid a bounty for his trip, which he needs in order to have enough money to marry Ethel Pepper. Fred, a big, burly man, built like a rugby forward, is already a veteran of the Great War. He walks with a slight limp, his left leg bent at an angle that gives him the nickname K-leg Corder. Somewhere in Flanders, he was shot through the knee and fell onto the barbed wire, providing a convenient human bridge for the others in his platoon to cross German lines.

Fred's father was a violent alcoholic, who despite an excellent job in the House of Commons, drank his family into poverty. Fred himself is prone to sudden and irrational mood swings. He enlisted in 1912, as soon as he was old enough to run away from his troubled home. He never speaks about his childhood, save to lecture his own children on the dangers of alcohol.

On the quayside, amongst the crowds of well-wishers gathered to cheer the ship on its way, is a slim local lad called Roland Wood. Roland is one of six children living in the then fashionable West End of Newcastle-upon-Tyne. He is training to be an architect. He too has served in the Great War, but as a volunteer. He now wears a moustache to hide the scars left by shrapnel wounds, sustained whilst a young Second Lieutenant in

Belgium, where he had been left for dead during a futile advance by the Northumberland Fusiliers. He has spent the last two years in and out of sanatoriums, fighting to regain the use of an arm that his father begged surgeons not to amputate.

Roland and Frederick were my grandfathers. They didn't meet on that day in 1919, but had to wait until 1951 when their youngest children, my parents, were married. The coincidence of that Newcastle quayside amused them. Both of them died young. I never knew Frederick and have only the faintest childhood memory of Roland.

The two men were ordinary lads; not untypical of their day and age.

One was fortunate to live in relative affluence at a time when most city-dwellers lived in conditions that would horrify us today - their house was one of the first to have electricity in Newcastle. The other was unfortunate to have been reared by a desperate, alcoholic brute. They probably had no realisation that they were living in extraordinary times. Both were lucky to have survived the greatest slaughter of young men in history.

Like Fred and Roland, we all leave a few doodles of our own across the margins of history. In Fred and Roland's case, there are some stiff, formal photographs, usually in uniform, a few medals, a cigarette box. In my study, I have the clever, well-drawn copies of Mickey Mouse, Pluto and Goofy that Roland drew for my mother's bedroom wall in the 1930's, that have been passed around the family for generations of young children to enjoy and somehow, as is the way in families, have found their way back to me. There's not much else.

Generations that follow us will find our names in the Census, on the deeds of properties, on electoral rolls, on membership lists in the archives of Trades Unions or professional bodies. We might have a box of keepsakes - the blazer badge, the school report condemning us as mediocre and lazy, a love letter, a certificate of baptism, a commemorative coin...

Not enough of us leave behind anything that will tell future generations what our lives were really like.

It doesn't matter that we are ordinary people doing ordinary things. A generation ago, it would have seemed the most outlandish idea that I could type this into a computer, using a keyboard. The next generation may find my method hysterically cumbersome, as they dictate their books into a computer. The generation afterwards will simply attach electrodes and "think" their words into a gadget smaller than a cigarette packet. In a hundred years time, someone will find this book in an antique shop selling such quaint items as books ("people used to read them you know") and laugh outrageously at just how wrong my predictions are.

Ordinary people are endlessly fascinating. Our lives may seem dull and trivial to us. Roland and Fred may well have believed theirs were too, but if they had only put down on paper some of their thoughts, if they had only taken a little time from their lives to write something about their experiences, we would know so much more.

Your life is not boring. You may not have climbed the Matterhorn or been to the moon or had a number one hit record. Most of us haven't. The biographies of the great and the good, the noisy, the powerful and the famous will always be recorded. The rest of us, the ordinary folk going about our ordinary daily lives are just as interesting - probably more so.

What you do every day will fascinate the generations to come.

Writing about your own life can't be that hard, can it? After all, it's **your** life, so you've got all the stories and characters to hand. You don't need to start inventing characters or plots - they're all there in your memories, your diaries, that little box of blazer badges and school reports.

When it comes down to it, you may well find it trickier than it looks.

Sometimes, it's hard to recall all the various events that make up our lives. There are the familiar faces with no names to go with them, there are the postcards in the attic from people you don't even remember. Dates, times and places melt into fuzzy, unfocused pictures.

Even when we can recall things clearly, actually getting that experience down can be a tough business. Have you ever tried writing down the anecdote that has your friends falling about laughing to find that it dies somewhere between the pen and the page?

This book is designed to help you write your life story. In it, there are suggestions to help you remember your past and to get your own story down on paper. Later in the book, I discuss various ways in which you can bring the story of your life to a wider audience.

In Chapter 8, I have provided several examples of autobiographical writing, not by the famous or well-to-do, but from men and women from ordinary walks of life who have set out to recall some of their experiences.

The examples I have chosen are from people I know from my work as a writing tutor. They are not professional writers, although many of them are easily good enough. They are from all walks of life - there are secretaries and nurses, teachers and office workers, people who've spent most of their lives on the factory floor, folk who've long since retired. Some of them have university degrees; others left school at fourteen or fifteen. Many had hardly written a thing since schooldays.

Above all, they have enthusiasm and this shines though in their writing.

So, if you want to tell your story

- for your own amusement
- as part of a family history
- for publication
- for friends
- for the nostalgia magazine market

- as a legacy for future generations
- as a few hundred words or a few hundred thousand
- to record your experiences of the war, old industries or a way of life that no longer exists,
- or simply to enjoy the act of writing

I hope that this book will help you to do it.

Nicholas Corder

Chapter 1 - What are you going to write?

....

"An Autobiography is a book a person writes about his own life and it is usually full of all sorts of boring details." Roald Dahl – Preface to his own autobiography "Boy".

Every one of us has a story to tell, so why not just get on with it?

Well, great, but before we simply jot down random thoughts and end up with a messy hotchpotch, let's take a little time to think about it.

I know there are some people who can just sit down at a desk and produce thousands of beautiful words that they will never have to change. They're the exception, not the rule. Most of us aren't like that.

After all, if you felt entirely confident that you could write your life story without any help whatsoever, you wouldn't be reading this book.

Before you even begin, it's worth asking yourself the simple, but crucial question "Why do I want to write this book?"

Yes, this may seem obvious, but why do you want to do it? After all, if you honestly intend writing something substantial, you are going to be taking up a good chunk of your life to do it.

There is another equally important question. Who is your audience? In fact, the two questions are intertwined; it's almost impossible to separate them, but I've tried. We'll look at the idea of audience shortly.

Why Write Your Story At All?

For fun?

We human beings love to be creative. Writing your life story is an absorbing way of tapping into the creative side of your personality. It's also remarkably inexpensive. You only need pen, paper and a little time. Add into that some will-power and you're well on your way to keeping yourself amused over several weeks, possibly months, even years.

I think that life stories written for the sheer fun of recording a life are often the best. You can tell when the writer has enjoyed their writing – it leaps off the page, involves you, makes you want to read on.

To Lay Ghosts to Rest?

All of us have been through events that trouble and disturb us. There are people we love who have died; we have broken marriages. We've done bad things to others, and been on the receiving end of a few raw deals ourselves. Some of us were traumatized by the most horrendous circumstances.

Often, writing about these events can be very therapeutic. The very act of getting them out of our heads and onto a sheet of paper can make us feel a great deal better. It's the equivalent of the confessional box or the psychiatrist's couch.

There's nothing wrong in this. "Writing out the demons" is a great idea. However, you do need to think who will actually want to read what you've written. If part of your reason for writing your life story was to let other people share your experiences, simply having a good moan for page after page is not going to keep them glued to your words. If what you want to write is the stuff of the psychiatrist's couch or the confessional, perhaps you need to re-think what you are doing.

To Get Your Own Back?

I can't imagine there can be anyone who has gone through life without someone being unpleasant to them at some stage. Wouldn't writing an autobiography and exposing the charlatans, cheats, bullies, back-stabbers and hypocrites be tremendous?

Again, I suspect this is a little like "writing out the demons". It could give you a great sense of release and renewed well-being. If published, it could also get you into serious trouble (see the section on libel). More importantly, writing a book as a means of getting your own back is unlikely to make for good reading.

No, if you want to get your own back, doing it in print is not the best way. Vindictiveness never looks good on paper. It makes the writer look worse than the original offender.

To tell an important part or episode of your life?

This is a very powerful reason for wanting to write your life story. You may simply want to tell the story of the years you spent in the army, or of your time as a land girl. Perhaps you were a nurse and want to show how things were in the old days. Maybe, you simply want to write about your travels – just think how much travel has changed, even in the last twenty years.

Once, even a trip from London to Paris was a huge adventure in exotica. Nowadays, the physical distance has been reduced by clever rail and aeroplane links.

Amongst the odd things I've collected over the years is a small hard-backed home-bound book of collated, type-written sheets, picked up at a car boot sale. There is a hand-written inscription in the front that reads "To Jane and George – Memories of a happy holiday in France, August, 1950".

Now, August 1950 is still within the living memory of a good number of folks. A trip to France seems like a commonplace event. However, there is the fascination of a world that has disappeared. As I write, Paris still exists, as does the Eiffel Tower, the Arc de Triomphe and the Champs Elysées, all of which get a good mention. Other things have altered dramatically.

We journey to France now by plane, car ferry, sea-cat, hovercraft or the channel tunnel. No longer is it a fourteen-plus hour trip on the overnight boat-train. The currency of France in the pages of the little home-bound book is the Franc (in fact, I suspect it may even be the old Franc), not the Euro. Nowadays, we can take as much money as we want in and out of France, but

16

those were the days of strict currency control. And who nowadays would spend an hour at a Bureau de Change waiting to cash travellers cheques to pay a hotel bill, when you can swipe it onto your credit card in under a minute? Whilst we might all still see what the last of our holiday small change might buy us, we are not limited to half a bottle of Benedictine and half a bottle of brandy when we get back to British Customs.

The audience for this particular little book is "Jane and George" – the friends of Sybil and the anonymous "I", author of the little journal. As such it is a testament to their friendship.

It may well be that you simply want to write something similar. I think this is a great idea. This particular little notebook is not of publishable quality. In fact, the author could have done with some of the tips in this book. However, it is based round one episode in someone's life. It is a record of their history and, as such, valid and valuable.

For Money?

Dr. Samuel Johnson is reported to have said "No man but a blockhead ever wrote, except for money."

I have to take issue with Dr. Johnson. The chap turning out for his local pub football team is playing football. He may not be playing at the same standard as the players in the national team (although you may sometimes wonder), and he's certainly not making their kind of money. Importantly, he is not expecting to be paid for his efforts. Nor is he considered a blockhead just because he fancies a game of football without the prospect of a match fee, a win bonus and the extensive use of a Ferrari.

There are plenty of things that can be done by professional and amateur alike. There is no reason why you have to make any money from your writing, unless of course you want to.

However, as soon as you start trying to earn money from your writing, you are stepping into a different league. I know that's sometimes hard to believe when you read some of the shoddiest efforts that somehow manage to wriggle their way into print, but you are. There's no point getting morose about this. There are untalented people in all walks of life – or perhaps, more accurately, there are people whose talents would be better served in other jobs. Writing is no exception.

I will deal with selling your writing later in this chapter and much more fully in chapter 7. For the moment, let me leave you with a thought. It is a little home truth, and one that you may not find particularly palatable.

What may be extremely interesting to you, your family and your friends may be of no interest whatsoever to people who do not know you.

If you want to sell your writing, you are going to have to appeal to people who do not know you at all.

After all, our pub footballer is, at best, expecting a couple of his mates and his girlfriend to come and cheer him on. He's not expecting a talent scout from Manchester United to come and sign him up whilst he's having his half-time cigarette. Writing is no different.

Who is your audience?
Just You?

Why not? What on earth is wrong in writing simply for yourself? There are plenty of people who are happy to dabble in watercolours without ever once wanting to display their efforts, even in the privacy of their own lavatory.

As I've already mentioned, writing is an engrossing hobby. You can learn a great deal writing only for yourself.

Your Family?

I suspect that the most common reason why people want to write their life stories is so that their families have a record of their lives. You can see from my introduction that I wish I had more information about my two grandfathers and their lives. Just think how fascinating it would be for someone a hundred years from now – perhaps one of your direct descendants - to come across a well-written document of your life.

The wider public?

It may be that you have greater ambitions for your work. If you do, more power to your elbow. There is nothing quite like the thrill of seeing your name in print. I once walked into a library that had twenty copies of a book of mine on the shelf and the thought of it gives me a buzz to this day. On the other hand, if I want to feel depressed, I can think of a couple of reviews that have left me feeling more than a little bruised.

Before you rush out and spend £1500 on the latest computer equipment because your autobiography's going to be a best-seller and such sums will soon be pocket-money, let me give you a little caveat. Getting a book published is hard work. Occasionally, there are memoirs or autobiographies written by unknown or obscure writers that become bestsellers. In the main, however, most publishers are not interested in autobiographies from unknowns.

You might write a classy little autobiography full of wit, warmth and wisdom that is turned down by every publishing house in the English-speaking world, only to find that the latest teen sensation, barely able to string two monosyllables together has been given a half-million pound advance for the story of his first (and only) twenty years.

It's not fair at all, but if you're old enough to be contemplating writing your life story, then you're probably old enough to accept the fact that life in general isn't fair.

I don't say this to put you off. If you've got a great story to tell and can tell it in a way that captures the reader's attention from the start, then you do stand a chance. I simply don't want to raise any false hopes.

A more realistic target may be to sell episodes from your life story to relevant publications.

Local Readers

Sometimes, you may find that your work does appeal to a wider public, but not to a nationwide one.

Stories of local interest can often find a home in local or regional magazines, but would never be considered by national publications.

Changing Ambitions

There's nothing wrong in deciding to write a few hundred words about the night your street was bombed during the Blitz and then deciding that you want to write about other aspects of your life as well. Nor is there anything wrong in trying to write an enormous 100,000 word biography and then deciding that really all you wanted to write about was the night your street was bombed during the blitz.

For the purposes of this book, we are imagining that you are going to write a work of 50,000 words. Of course, that's just pretend. In fact, it doesn't matter if you're writing a handful of episodes or an entire life story – the techniques and tips in this book will help you to do both.

It's a big adventure. You will remember things that you'd long confined to the dusty attic of your mind. You will discover things about yourself, your friends and family that you had never realised before.

But before you set off on this journey, remind yourself. You're doing it for the fun of it. Writing is absorbing, fascinating, involving. At times, it can also be infuriating, when you realise that either the words won't flow or what you've written is below par.

Don't panic. This happens to everyone. I don't think you can avoid these hiccoughs and barren patches completely. However, the way to cut down on them is to plan what you are going to write. Planning is the subject of our next chapter.

Chapter 2 - Planning Your Book

....

"We shall not cease from exploration
And the end of all our exploring
Will be to arrive where we started
And know the place for the first time" T.S. Eliot, Little Gidding,

Recently, by the glories of the internet, I have been re-united with several friends from my teenage years.

My old mate Nick manages an insurance company and Dave has built up his own clothing business. My teenage sweetheart, Lydia, now edits a children's magazine in Canada. Suddenly, after a gap of 25 + years, they have sprouted children, many of whom are at least as old as we were when we were last in contact.

None of us has been a polar explorer, visited the moon, won a Nobel prize. We have all led "normal" lives, managing to stay out of gaol (harder for some than for others) and are entering our comfortable middle years with our minds more intact than our hairlines or waistlines.

Yet, we have all achieved things in our own small ways. We have moved on. We are no longer the raw callow youths we once were. We have changed. We have new responsibilities and new freedoms. Whilst something of the people we were then remains in us, we are also different in many ways.

We have new friends. We've had partners, lovers, motor accidents, brushes with death, bereavements, broken marriages, children. We now have a history. It may only be 25 years ago, but in those years the world has seen artificial insemination, cloning, AIDS, The Falklands and Gulf Wars. We can now even tell the difference between butter and margarine.

Where once we would crowd into someone's bedroom and listen to the latest vinyl LP, we have CDs, minidisks and music that can be downloaded from the internet. We have mobile phones. Our school didn't have a computer back then. Now all four of us owns at least one.

In all that time trouser bottoms and ties have narrowed and then widened again. Punk rock came and went. They gave all the bad boys of rock music knighthoods. The Queen had another jubilee. Almost anything that moves (or in the case of the railways, doesn't) has been privatised. Surgery is done through a key-hole. They've stopped sending men to the moon. We love the Russians and they love us enough to buy our football teams.

In amongst all these enormous changes, how do we set about describing our lives to one another?

Look on a website such as Friends Reunited and you'll see little summaries of the lives of old school friends trying to get in touch with one another. Each one condenses years of lives into a few bald statements about "new" families, wives and husbands we'd never met and our current work. They read along the following lines "I'm still working at the bank. I have a wonderful husband and two children," or "I still see Charlie Snodgrass from time to time".

It seems somehow too bland for us to condense so much into a couple of paragraphs. Yet, when you ask yourself a question such as "what have I done in the last 10/25/50 years" it gets a bit awkward. We sketch our lives in the briefest of outlines. Wrack our brains though we might, most of us will be able to point to only a handful of major live events. Somehow, we've only got the skeletons of our lives to talk about, but if we are going to write in any depth about our lives, we need the flesh to put on that skeleton.

The biggest problem is that the memory is a funny beast. It's always playing tricks on you. One moment you think you've grasped hold of some tenuous fragment of your earlier life and then it's gone.

If you're anything like me, you can still quote large passages of poetry you were made to learn by heart at school, but can't remember the name of the person you've just been introduced to.

Even describing how the memory works is difficult. Sometimes, you can think of your memory as being a sort of Emmentaler cheese with more holes than cheese – memories fall through the holes.

Or maybe it's a bit more like an old muslin bag that you use for straining jam. Some memories squeeze through the little rips that have appeared over the years and are gone, but there are some bits that cling tenuously here and there to the gauze of the bag.

Or perhaps it's a bit like having a rather ineffectual shredder. Your memories are all written on sheets of paper and they are passed through the shredder. Some pieces come out virtually intact, others are in large pieces, but can still be stuck together; others still are too fragmentary, or simply become paper dust at the bottom of the shredder.

Whatever description you prefer – and if you don't like any of those descriptions, make one up for yourself – I'm sure you'll agree that even those of us with the clearest, strongest, most comprehensive memories need reminding about things from time to time.

How Can I Remember Everything I Need To Write My Book?

You can't. It's impossible for us to remember everything that has happened to us in our lives. Given that we can't remember everything, what we need are some tools for helping us to stretch our memories to bring to mind as much as we can.

In this section of the chapter, I'm going to suggest some techniques you could use to help you to get your memories working well.

Everyone has his or her own way of doing anything. What I don't want to suggest is that there is only one way of approaching any of the aspects of life story writing. That includes memory-techniques, so please feel free to use, adapt, ignore or develop ideas of your own, so that you come up with a range of techniques to suit yourself.

Using Memorabilia

Some people are amongst nature's hoarders. They squirrel away every last memento of their lives, right down to bus tickets and notes to the milkman.

Others are bleak minimalists, shedding every tiny scrap of everything remotely personal.

Most of us hover somewhere on the continuum between these two extremes.

I'm not a great one for keeping much in the way of bits from my past. Every now and again, I have a good clear out on the basis that I'm using parts of my house for storage that might be better put to use as living space. Nevertheless, I do still have my school reports (just to remind myself what an idle soul I am at heart), a couple of scrapbooks of the minor achievements of my life, a couple of photo albums and an archive of all the articles, stories, books and plays I've written and had published (it's sad, but it's my only claim to fame). For some reason, I've also got a fabulous collection of rejection slips and letters. Old diaries, address books, postcards, letters and programmes from plays, football and cricket matches have long been consigned to the recycling bin. Even so, I've still got enough personal bric à brac to start putting together the story of my life.

If you are better at keeping personal records than I am, then you are in an even stronger position. Look, for years you've been keeping all that stuff, swearing that one day it would come in handy, and now it can!

Perhaps you are the kind of person who can maintain a diary religiously and keep all your birthday and Christmas cards. Perhaps you have drawers full of old correspondence. Perhaps you have scrapbooks and photo albums – maybe the photos even have captions.

Whatever you do have – it is a really good idea to gather your personal archive from around the house and spread it out over a table somewhere.

Useful material you could gather would include:
- Diaries
- School reports
- Letters & postcards
- Photos
- Poems that someone in your family has written
- Old address books
- Thumbnail sketches of old friends (can be got from Internet sites, such as Friends Reunited)
- Programmes from plays, sports events
- Certificates, trophies or any prizes you have won
- Cuttings from the local newspaper
- The family tree

Simply browsing through all this material is bound to start the memory juices flowing.

Look at an old school photo, and although you're unlikely to be able to name everyone on it, you'll suddenly find the name of some long-forgotten classmate springs back into your mind. Similarly, if you dig out an old school report, you'll be reminded of your teachers. Who were the tyrants who left you trembling in the corridor? Who were the gentle ones you were horrid to? Who were the inspiring ones who turned you on to a lifetime's interest in their subject?

Talking About the Past

Another good way of remembering your past is by simply talking about it. If you have brothers or sisters, I am sure you will be able to chat about childhood events. If you can, try to find people from your past – for instance old school friends – and have a little reunion with them. You'll be amazed at how many memories are prompted by simply gossiping over a drink or two at a pub.

I was recently involved in a fascinating project involving people talking about their lives. As late as the 1970s, women were employed at the pitheads of Cumbrian coalmines. Their job was to sort the coal from a conveyor belt, removing any rocks and impurities.

The project involved collecting the oral histories of these women whose lives had been hard, tough and uncompromising. As they sat round the table talking of their past lives, almost everything that was said triggered an associated memory. Soon there was a bubbling hubbub of reminiscence taking place. Just a handful of two-hour sessions provided enough material for both a book recording their working lives and a play based on their experiences.

Using Topic Headings

Another way to stir the memories is quite simply to jot down a few notes under a particular heading. Here are some that you might like to use. Obviously, some might not apply to you, and there may well be others that you would want to add.

- Accidents and Disasters
- Ambitions
- Arguments
- Birth
- Breaking The Law
- Brothers & Sisters
- Career
- Chance Happenings
- Children
- Christmas, Easter, Hogmanay, Etc.
- College
- Death Of Someone Who Was Close To You
- Disappointments

- Dreams
- Everyday Disasters
- Famous people
- First Communion/Confirmation
- First Day At School/College/Work
- First Home
- First Impressions
- First Job
- First Love
- Four Seasons – Spring, Summer, Autumn, Winter
- Friends
- Games
- Grandparents
- Hobbies
- Holidays
- Illnesses
- Marriage
- Money
- Neighbours
- Obsessions
- Parents
- Pets
- Politics
- Possessions
- Religion
- Romance
- School
- Shopping
- Somewhere you Know Well
- Sports
- Strong Characters
- Teachers
- Teenagers
- Tough Decisions

- Triumphs and Successes
- University
- War/Service In The Forces

Superlatives

You may have noticed that in the last section several of the topic headings start with the word "first". First is a superlative, and thinking in terms of superlatives is a useful idea at the planning stage.

You might consider writing about any or all of the following:

- My best teacher
- My favourite pet
- My most frightening experience
- My worst day
- My earliest memory
- My best holiday
- My favourite book
- My worst boss
- My first car
- My strangest dream
- My biggest nightmare
- My worst fear

I'll stop the list there. If you're going to use this technique, you will probably want to write your own headings.

Once you have started stirring the memories, you will want to start keeping notes. Don't worry at this stage about how neat these notes are. They are notes for you, not for anyone else. One of the great things about writing is that nobody needs to see how messy the process is; it's the end product that counts.

Try to jot things down as they occur to you. Yet again, don't worry about how scruffy these notes are. The important thing at this stage is to be collecting material - the kernels of ideas, if you like - not worrying about how many marks your old English teacher would have given you for your handwriting.

If you do want to start getting your notes into some kind of order, it's quite a good idea to invest in either a good, strong thick A4-sized notebook where you can start labelling the pages with appropriate headings, or better still, why not buy one of those A-Z concertina files? Then, you can label each section appropriately and put notes, pictures or any other memorabilia into its relevant section.

Alternatively, or even additionally, if you have the wall space, a pin-board is ideal. I have an enormous pin-board that I often use as a planning device. I use it for larger projects and it normally ends up covered in pictures, post-it notes, bits of paper and snippets of ideas. The great thing about a pin-board is that it allows you to see an overall picture of where your work is heading.

Whilst you might be able to write an episode from your life, or even an entire chapter of a book at one sitting, you're not going to be able to do a whole book in one go.

Using a pin-board is one way of giving you a visual guide as to how all those little separate episodes join up.

You could equally well using the dining-table, but the drawback with that is that you have to clear everything away every time you want to sit down for a meal.

Pre-writing

You should now be at the stage where you have started to collect a great deal of material and you should be itching to turn these memories into scintillating prose.

You may be one of those people who simply likes to get straight down to the task of writing. Again, this is perfectly fine. There are no rules for how you set about writing the story of your life.

However, some of us, if we sit down to write with no notes, nothing on a piece of paper to guide us, feel lost. We feel as though we've been set down on some Lake District Mountain without map, compass, guide (or even Kendal Mint Cake).

If you are one of that brave band who can simply sit down with a pad of paper, or flick on the computer and start working with no worries as to what you are going to write, then I envy you, as will 90% of the people reading this.

If, like me, you don't feel confident about starting anything without at least some idea of where you're going, then some sort of pre-writing is essential.

I like to jot down just a handful of ideas and notes before I start writing anything. These notes are just for me. I don't think anyone else would find them legible, let alone make any sense of them. As I am essentially disorganised by nature and you need to be well organised in order to write, I conquer my natural tendency to chaos by having a notebook for each project I am doing. I tend to buy spiral-bound, plastic-covered notebooks in either A4 or A5 size, depending on the project. I also keep a plastic folder for each job into which I put early drafts of my work and copies of any research materials I have. Plastic folders last longer and can be re-used for the next job.

There is no order to my work. Notes sprout on any page that comes to hand, but this is a simple way of keeping everything together.

That's just me. I write professionally and always have a dozen or more projects on the go at any one time, so it's my way of conquering my disorderliness.

Another useful concept that you might like to consider is the idea of "marinating". In the same way as you might leave a piece of meat to soak in a sauce for some time, you can leave an idea or a fragment of a story to stew in the juices of the mind. For generations, psychologists and psychiatrists and anyone who can hold a clipboard and wear a white coat have been trying to work out how the human subconscious works. Don't worry yourself about how it works, just accept the fact that it does. In the same way that you come wide awake in the middle of the night with the words "Alma Cogan" – the name you couldn't remember over dinner earlier that evening – so too will fragments of memory join up.

It's an incredibly strong technique to use, but don't expect it to work all the time. As with all things to do with the mind, your brain won't work with circuit board logic and you will still find that you haven't got a clue what the name of the woman who lived next door was called, no matter how long you leave it to marinate.

Dividing your work into chapters

There is no way in which you can write your book in one sitting. There is also no way in which a reader can read your book without it being divided into manageable chunks. Knowing how to divide your work is quite a skill.

One way of organising your book is arithmetical. We have already decided that the book is 50,000 words long, so what's wrong with dividing the book into ten chapters, each of around 5,000 words? That keeps the maths simple.

Of course, it won't work as easily as that, but you might find that the idea that each chapter should be around the 5,000 word mark will help you to make the book feel balanced. On the other hand, there's also no reason why you should have ten chapters. Why not 14 or 17 or 20? There's also no earthly reason why chapters have to be of the same length. In the book you are holding, for instance, the shortest chapter is around half the length of the longest.

However, concentrating on chapter length actually takes us away from the real issue of how to divide the book. It's not always a simple question of arithmetic; you need to develop a feel for which bits fit with one another.

There are as many approaches to this as there are autobiographies written. For the sake of this book, I am going to suggest that there are two main ways of going about dividing your book.

The first approach is to work in some kind of chronological order. You simply start with your earliest memories and work up to the point where you have decided to end your story.

The second is to divide your life into topics or themes. If you are writing a chronological account, then your chapter headings might be something like:

- Early life
- School days
- National service - Malaya
- Working for the company
- Family life
- Big promotion and the big move
- Life in the boardroom
- Working for myself
- Retirement
- Where I am now

On the other hand, you might like to go for an approach that is more "thematic" and is based not just around the events of your life, but also around interests and enthusiasms.

In this case, your chapter headings might be something like:

- Mother
- Education
- DIY
- Holidays
- Climbing the corporate ladder
- Our house
- Children and grandchildren
- My obsession with football
- Church

Of course, these approaches are bound to overlap. For instance, let's suppose that you take the thematic approach. You will probably find that the chapter dealing with your education is chronological. You start with primary school and finish when, late in life, you are awarded your Open University degree.

One of the best ways of finding out how you want your book to be divided up is to get hold of an autobiography that you have particularly enjoyed. Re-read it, noting down how the author divides the work, then try to use the same approach in your own work.

How Long Is It Going To Be?

Throughout this book, we are imagining that the project you are embarked on is a book of 50,000 words.

This is only so that I, the writer, and you, the reader, share some idea of the kind of task that's in store for you.

The reality is that you have to decide how long your work is going to be.

If you are hoping that your finished manuscript will be published, it is more likely that your book will need to be longer than the suggested 50,000 words. In fact, few publishers are likely to look at anything shorter than around 80,000 words and, indeed, 100,000 words is a more realistic target.

On the other hand, if you are writing for your own amusement and that of your family and close friends, then the manuscript can be any length you chose to make it. In fact, the danger of trying to write 100,000 words is that you spin your tale out too thinly and are left with far too much padding.

If you are less experienced as a writer, then you might find that you are better off keeping your ambitions modest to begin with. You might like to concentrate on just one period in your life. Then, if you find that your words are starting to flow, you can expand your ambitions as you go along and start writing about other facets of your life. If you start with the grand ambition of writing a full-blown book of 100,000 words and find that you only manage 30,000, it is easy to view this as failure.

On the other hand, if you decide simply to write up a few episodes and then discover that you have a work of 30,000 words, it can feel like a grand success. Of course, in reality, you've produced the same number of words whichever way you look at it, but doesn't the second approach taste more like success than the first?

Now we've got a few jottings and notes together, let's see about doing some real writing.

Chapter 3 - Getting Started and Keeping Going

....

"We never do anything well till we cease to think about the manner of doing it." William Hazlitt

Climbing Mount Everest Without A Sherpa

We've decided that your book will be 50,000 words long. If it's the first time you've ever written anything that long, it looks like a long, daunting haul. 50,000 words! How on earth am I ever going to do it? It's like climbing Mount Everest without a Sherpa.

It's at this stage that you may start looking round for some excuses not to get down to writing. These may range from the highly practical "I must clean the cooker" to the pseudo-arty "I don't feel as though the muse is on me today."

You can prepare to write forever. If you are ever going to get anything written, then one day you must actually sit down and start. It's that obvious, really.

If it's any consolation to you, every writer I know has huge tussles with themselves and their consciences before they get down to any serious work. One friend of mine says that you can always tell when he has to write something, because you'll find him cleaning the house. He's not the world's most house-proud man either, so when cleaning beats writing, you know that writing must be hard work.

Well, it is … and it isn't. Writing is not the same kind of hard work as being a North Sea trawlerman, coal miner, social worker in a tough neighbourhood, police officer or soldier in battle. All these jobs are a lot harder than just sitting at the computer keyboard and flailing away with a couple of fingers for an hour or so. Most writers would agree that the toughest part of being a writer is the self-discipline – the sitting down and keeping going.

The book you hold in your hands contains approximately 38,000 words – a little shorter than your story will be. That's still a lot of words. It's not "War and Peace", but it's still a fair number and, with the exception of a few short samples of writing in Chapter 8, I've had to write all of them. Frankly, I'm amazed I've done it. I'm an idle so-and-so, really.

If I can write a book (and, excluding plays, this is my third), so can you. My school reports (yes, kept in that famous box in the loft) are littered with such phrases as "lacks self-discipline", "works well, but only when pushed" or "he has shown no effort whatsoever this year". I promise you that I have to chain myself to my desk to get anything done at all.

Don't be put off as you gaze towards that 50,000 word summit. There are several techniques, tricks and ideas that you can use. Think of them as your own little writing Sherpas.

Break the Job Down Into Smaller Chunks

When you start with a blank page or computer screen, the task looks formidable. When you think that you're going to have to write tens of thousands of words, you'll probably want to snap this book shut and slope off to watch Coronation Street or Eastenders.

I don't know about you, but I do like a chocolate biscuit. I couldn't eat a wholesale size box of them at a single sitting, but if I managed a couple each day, eventually I'd have eaten the whole box.

Instead of thinking of your book as one big job, break it down into smaller ones. This book is divided into chapters. The chapters are then sub-divided into topics and themes. If I try to write the book at one sitting, I'll never write it. If I break it down into parts, then it makes the job easier and a lot less daunting.

If you're going to write a life story of 50,000 words and decide you can write about 500 words a day, then in 100 days time (a little over three months), you will have a rough draft. If you can manage 1,000 words a day, then you'll have a complete rough draft in around seven to eight weeks.

Sure, it will need revising and checking and there'll be bits you hate and have to change, but at least you will have something to work from.

For each chunk of writing you do, promise yourself a small bribe. Award yourself a cup of coffee when you get to the end of the page. Yes, you could wander off and get one at any stage, but until you reach the bottom of that page, you're not going to have one.

Get the Writing Habit

After we leave school, most of our writing tends to be work-related, if we write at all. Our English becomes mangled by the demands of writing reports, specification documents, email.

On the rare occasions when we do write something a little more creative, we probably do so in a flash of inspiration when a great idea occurs to us.

Professional writers write every day. They get into the habit of making sure they are inspired the moment their bottom hits the seat. They can't afford to wait until the muse condescends to pay them a fleeting visit.

So, get the writing habit. It's like anything: the more you practise, the easier it becomes. It will seem less like a chore if you manage to make a short burst of writing part of your daily routine.

Finding the Time to Write

Given the fact that we have machines to do our washing, washing-up, clean our carpets, take us to work and perform so many other tasks that would have taken our forebears days to do, why is it we always seem to be squeezed for time in the modern world.

Even when people retire, they're constantly amazed at how much time their various activities take up. A common cry is "I don't know how I found the time to work." If they found the time to work, they can certainly find the time to write.

Yes, but there are family commitments, work pressures and you want time simply to relax. Agreed, but if you look at your weekly schedule, I am sure that you can find some slots in which to write. You don't have to set aside hours at a time - in fact you might find that in three slots of fifteen minutes, you get just as much work done as you do in one slot of an hour.

If you can set aside longer periods to do some writing, then do so. I use the first couple of hours in the morning for writing. I also try to get an extra hour's uninterrupted writing at some point in the early evening, but I regard it as a bonus if I get something done then. During my writing periods, I break off every 30-40 minutes, have a coffee, check my email, make a few notes and so on. I try to relegate all the other bits of my work to later in the day. It doesn't always work out that way, but at least that's my intention. Yes, I know I write more-or-less full-time, but there was a stage when I had a proper job and slotted it in.

If you need to "make" time, then there are ways it can be done.

Television eats into our lives enormously. We often just switch it on for a bit of background noise. I actually like television and think that, if you are discriminating in your viewing, there is plenty of good stuff. One way to stop it encroaching on your writing time is to record the programmes you want to watch and view them later. You'll be surprised how many TV programmes you "just had to watch" languish for months, unviewed, when recorded onto video tape.

Clean the house a little less often, mow the lawn when it needs it, not just because it's Sunday. Make the kids or your spouse do more than they normally do.

Get up half-an-hour early and write during that time, before the rest of the household is awake.

Force everyone out of the house one afternoon a week and use that time to write.

If you're still struggling to find time, then get yourself a book on time management or, if you prefer, simply record everything you do in a week and look for little gaps you could use. Remember, your writing "slot" does not have to be a huge amount of time. Write a hundred words in ten minutes and you are making progress. Write nothing in two hours, and you're not.

When you're writing, one nifty trick is to remove your wristwatch. If you've got a little clock on the corner of your computer screen, cover it up. If you've got one on the wall or shelf, turn it round. Many of us have the bad habit of looking at our watches all the time. I'm convinced that looking at your watch when writing actually physically slows down the earth's rotation, so everything takes longer.

Writing Space

If you have a room you can set aside for writing, then that is ideal. If you're not fortunate enough to have such a place, then you're probably going to have to make do with a corner of a bedroom or even the kitchen. If you are a wandering soul, you might like to write in different places around the house. Some people adore writing longhand in cafés with the hubbub of strangers around them. One of my friends goes and sits in the caravan in her garden for peace and quiet. Another of my students recently bought a garden shed, just to write in.

Many of us like a fairly fixed place to work. It's good to be able to spread your work out on a table or a desk and not to have to worry too much about how tidy it looks.

Whatever you opt for, make sure you use that space as often as you can.

The Mechanics of Writing

Some people swear blind that unless they use an antique fountain pen, handmade paper and purple ink squeezed from the shells of the female Akhbar beetle, found only in the deepest jungle of Sarawak, they cannot wring out a single word. Others use an old ballpoint and the backs of envelopes. Some writers swear by their ancient portable typewriters; some work directly onto a word-processor or computer.

Frankly, it doesn't much matter which method you adopt. I type directly onto a computer, because I get cramp in my hand if I write longhand and, never having learned to type properly, I can't copy-type. For me, copy typing involves having to look at a piece of paper and a keyboard, whereas typing from my head means I only have to look at the keyboard. From time to time, I glance up to the screen to make sure that my words are appearing on it and no dreadful electronic catastrophe has frozen the beast several paragraphs ago.

Do Not Disturb

Ring-fence your writing time and space. If you plan to write on Thursday evening from 8.00 till 10.00, then put it in your diary, exactly as you would an appointment. If anyone wants you to do something on Thursday evening, you have to turn them down, no matter what. You are only allowed to break this rule if it's Michelle Pfeiffer on her knees in a negligée waving World Cup Final tickets or George Clooney with tickets for Wimbledon Centre court or some equivalent.

Don't answer the phone. If you can't appoint anyone to answer it on your behalf, invest in an answer phone. I know they cost money and you may end up returning a phone call to another hemisphere, but at least you'll be writing.

Banish all members of the family from wherever it is you have chosen as your writing space. If you make your writing time fairly short and to a regular pattern, then it is easier not to have it disturbed. Stress to them how important a project this is for you.

Buy one of those signs for the front door that warn anyone trying to sell you anything that you keep Pit Bulls, Rottweilers, a pride of free-range lions and an electric cattle prod that you reserve for anyone attempting to sell you anything door-to-door.

If a campaigning politician comes to the door asking if they can count on your vote, tell them they can. This rule holds no matter what your politics, their politics or the overwhelming desire you have to let loose the Pit Bulls, Rottweilers and lions or have a real go at them with that cattle prod.

Editing Brain versus Writing Brain

Many writers have commented about there being two halves of the writer's personality. First, there is the free-flowing part that allows you to crack on with writing. Then there is the editorial, censoring, checking part that nags constantly and says things like:

- You don't spell it like that!
- You can't put that!
- You've already said that!
- You've used that word three times in the same sentence!
- Somebody's written that kind of thing before!

Often, we find that we block ourselves from writing, simply because Editing Brain takes control and pooh-poohs everything we're trying to do.

The trouble with criticising what you are writing too early on is that your writing isn't ready for it. I never show a first draft of anything I write to anyone. I advise students to do the same. More often than not, first drafts are always messy, full of broken sentences, poor grammar, questionable spelling, and half-formed ideas. Mine look like the crazed scribblings of an orang-utan on acid.

Now, Editorial Brain is a useful chap to have, but you don't want him interfering whilst you're just trying to write. You want to use the free-flowing Writing Brain.

Writing Brain simply forges ahead, getting all the work down on paper. Editing Brain can only carp and correct. He's a bit like a critic. And let's face it, as Brendan Behan said, "Critics are like eunuchs in a harem: they know how it's done, they've seen it done every day, but they're unable to do it themselves."

Keep Editing Brain out of the way at the moment. I'll show you how to use him effectively in Chapter 5.

Don't even stop to check dates, spellings or precise facts unless they make a real difference to your story. It's just too easy to get side-tracked.

Is it spelled "Springbock" or "Springbok"? Oh, now that's interesting, there's something called Spring Canker Worm - they're a kind of caterpillar and they can destroy an entire orchard, I hope I haven't got them - oh, no it's just in parts of the United States. So what's this Spring Vetch, then? It's a kind of weed or tare. Weren't tares in the parable of the sower? Let's have a look, then. No, it doesn't seem to be that one. Where did I put the family bible? Now, weeds and tares, that rings a bell. Can't find it. My mother might know. Yes, hello, Mum. Yes I know I phoned yesterday, but …Oh, she's not is she? So how did that happen? No, I'll ring her straight away…..

Before you know it, your writing session has ended up as something else altogether. If you need to find something out later, either jot it on a piece of paper, highlight it in your handwritten text with a highlighter pen or, if you're typing onto a computer, type in "xx". When you come to check your work, simply click on "Find" and enter "xx" and then you can work at putting in the correct spelling, information, date, whatever.

Don't be frightened to go where your mind takes you if it's at least relevant to your writing. If you suddenly find yourself flipping from one idea to another, just write them down, or at least jot down a couple of notes for writing up later. As I write this, I have my notebook open on my desk and am working intermittently on three chapters at the same time. I'm allowing my Writing Brain to do the work. I can tidy it all up later.

Keep a Progress Chart

Do a progress chart. I do two for each book I write. It's a childish ploy to give me a sense of achievement.

One of them is a simple word count. Every time I finish a writing session, I block out how many words I've added since the last session. I actually do mine on the computer, but you can also do a simple wall chart and shade in the squares using different coloured pencils, then you can judge how many words you are averaging in a session. The other is a chapter-by-chapter word count, so that I get a feeling that the book is balanced and that the chapters are of a sensible length.

Music

If you find it useful to have music playing in the background, then do so. Stephen King goes in for heavy metal music. Some writers find modern songs distracting. Baroque music or Gregorian chant are my personal favourites. I don't really listen to them, it's just that they cover those unwholesome silences when the keyboard isn't clattering.

Don't Expect What You Write to Be a Work of Genius

Let's be blunt. If you were going to win the Nobel Prize for Literature, you'd probably be well on your way now. You wouldn't be reading this book. I'm not going to win it either - which is why I'm writing the book.

J.B. Priestley said "Write as often as possible, not with the idea at once of getting into print, but as if you were learning an instrument."

You can't expect to pick up a violin one week and be soloing with the London Philharmonic the next. Writing is a skill that needs some practice. There is no reason why, with a little exercise, you can't produce good, polished writing. You're unlikely to produce it at your first attempt, though.

Make Some Writing Friends

Writing is a solitary activity. In extreme cases it can lead to real isolation. If you are at all sociable by nature, try to make sure that you also do plenty of socialising in between writing sessions.

You may find it worth your while to mix with other writers. You could join a writers' group, writers' circle or enrol on a local adult education course. If you find that a regular weekly commitment is difficult, look out for one-day courses or short residential courses such as those organised by the Arvon Foundation or the Adult Residential Colleges Association. See Appendix B for a list of these organisations.

Find a writing partner. By that I don't mean someone who will co-write your book, but someone who is on a similar wavelength to you. Many people find it useful, exhilarating and encouraging to get-together from time to time over a cup of coffee to discuss progress, each others' work and to escape from the loneliness of writing. But don't use it as an excuse not to do any real writing.

Read, Read, Read

Read as much as you can. There are some wonderful autobiographies and memoirs out there. Browse your local bookshop and library shelves. Get out as many as you can and read them. Work out just what it is about a book that you like or dislike. There is a list of these books that I've enjoyed over the years in Appendix A. You will doubtless have favourites of your own. Remember that bad writing is worth reading as much as good writing. It shows us useful mistakes and it also makes us say "Hang on a minute. I could do better than that."

Writers' Block

Some people reckon that this doesn't exist. I'm not sure. It's hard to write if you've suffered some kind of personal tragedy, but I suspect that most "writer's block" is just a variation in output. I'm not quite sure why writers are particularly affected by this. After all sewage workers don't get toilet block, carpenters don't get wood block, drivers don't get road block and mechanics don't get engine block. Perhaps it means that you can put your hand to your fevered brow and go "But, darling, I'm an artist!"

Maybe that's too flippant. Ask any writer and they will tell you that there are some days when every word feels like they're passing a gallstone, and yet there are other days when time flies by and, instead of the 500 words they had promised to write, they've managed half a book. I had a miserable day yesterday squeezing out words like the last of a toothpaste tube, today I've written most of this chapter. Accept the fact that you're unlikely to write the same amount at each writing session.

On the days when the words don't flow, it can be a most upsetting experience.

Here are some tricks you can use to get yourself writing. First, write anything - a shopping list, a postcard to Auntie Flo, a letter to an old school friend, a note to the milkman. Imagine that you are a world-famous writer and that these little scraps of your genius will one day be auctioned for unheard-of sums.

If you're still stuck, try looking out of the window. As I write, my neighbour is busy self-building a house and is depositing piles of sand all over the place. I can see the outline of the new house in the footings. I can guess from them what each of the rooms is going to be - a bedroom, a living room, a garage, whatever. What can you see from yours? Note the colours, the shapes, any people or animals or movement you can see. Start writing down anything you can.

Do something different. If you've got a dog, walk it. Take a letter down to the post office, go for a ride on a bus or a train. Drive to a place you like. Go to a café with your notebook and jot down anything about the people around you.

Get hold of a truly badly written book and cheer yourself up in the confident knowledge that you can write better than that.

Leave a sentence half-finished, so that next time you come to write you are at least part way through your first sentence of the day.

Do something else that is connected with your writing. For instance, you could try to make a list of everyone who was in the netball team at school, what toys you owned as a child, the weddings you have been to, who worked with you in your first job, all your teachers in Primary School.

Alternatively, pick out a few old photographs and try to remember where they were taken or if each has a little story.

Look through your old address books to see if any of the old names stir up memories.

Instead of thinking of it as "writing time lost", try to think of it as some other kind of time gained. File some paperwork, write some cheques, clean the kitchen floor. Do any of the little jobs that you've been waiting to do. No, you won't get any writing done, but at least your house won't be as messy.

Make sure that your writer's block isn't simply caused by setting yourself unrealistic targets. Have a look at the number of words you are expecting to write in a session and revise them if you think you're being over-ambitious.

If you're really still stuck - give up for a few days. There is no point in forcing the issue. If the words genuinely won't flow, then you're only depressing yourself by not achieving anything. Leave it for a while. Your writing ability will return.

Don't worry if It's Been Done Before

Evelyn, who joined a weekly class of mine several weeks after it had started, was hoping to write about her life as a district nurse. When she discovered that another student, Rita, was also writing about her experiences as a nurse, she was worried that she wouldn't be able to do it. After all, wouldn't she just be writing exactly the same thing?

As it happens, although they did similar work, Rita's story is set in the harsh, poverty-stricken streets of early 1960's South London. Evelyn's idea was for a rural tale of Cumbrian farmers, with life at a slower pace. Although both Evelyn and Rita write well and with warmth, humour and perception about the people they meet, they are two different people, so their stories come out very differently.

Remember - everything anybody writes has been written before. There are no new stories, but there are variations on a theme. The fact that YOU are writing it is what makes it different.

If you were to ask a happily married couple to write about their wedding day, you would get two entirely different accounts of what is the same event.

Once you've run out of excuses as to why you can't write, the time has come to get on with the writing.

How Do the Real Writers Do It?

New writers often feel that there can only be one way to write a book. They want to know exactly how a writer gets down to the task in hand. Once they have the secret of how to sit down and write, then the words will flow.

The public perception of writers is that they swan out of bed well after sunrise, mix themselves a campari-soda to take away the taste of last night's champagne, perhaps do a spot of marlin fishing off the Florida Keys, then it's back home to knock out a few pages of witty and perceptive dialogue, before a dinner-suited first night of their West End play. Otherwise it's six-hour lunches with agents and publishers, whilst their personal stockbrokers relay them hot-tips for the Next Big Thing.

Of course, there's nothing like a fantasy to get in the way of reality. In the main, writers just get on with the job, using whatever method suits them best.

Stephen King writes in the mornings, leaving his afternoons free for business matters and sleep and the evenings free for his family.

The late Barbara Cartland would drape herself along one of her pink sofas and dictate her books at the speed of sound to at least one of her four secretaries.

Joseph Heller, author of the great "Catch 22", wrote his masterpiece by getting up early in the morning before commuting to his job as an advertising copywriter.

Roald Dahl, one of the most popular children's authors of all time, who had certainly made a great deal of money and could easily have afforded the poshest of offices, continued to work in his garden shed with a wooden board on his blanket-swathed knees, writing long-hand in pencil.

James Herriot wrote in the evenings, after work, in the middle of his family with the television blaring and he didn't fare badly with his autobiographical books at all.

Jack Kerouac wrote "On the Road" on an old typewriter, using a continuous roll of paper, so that he didn't have to waste time re-loading individual sheets. Apparently he wrote it in two weeks - but that's Benzedrine for you.

There are as many ways of writing as there are writers. There is no "right" way to set about your task. Simply find out what works for you and do it. The more often you do it, the easier it will become.

So let's use the next chapter to look at some writing techniques you can apply to your life story.

Chapter 4 - Writing Techniques for the Life Story Writer

....

"Great literature is the creation, for the most part, of disreputable characters, many of whom looked rather seedy, some of whom were drunken blackguards, a few of whom were swindlers or perpetual borrowers, gamblers or slaves to a drug." Alexander Harvey

When we write, we have a duty not to bore our readers. If we bore them, we'll soon lose them. If you're going to put in all this effort, you want someone to read the results, don't you?

A great way of making your writing stronger and more colourful is to think like a fiction writer, rather than like an "autobiographer". There is no reason why you can't use many of the techniques that novelists use to hook their readers and make their books exciting.

In this chapter, I will give you some ideas about how to do this. So what follows are some methods and a few examples. You might like to try them out for yourself. You will soon find that they become an automatic part of your writing, making your story livelier and more interesting.

If you don't like my examples, then that's great. Set yourself the challenge of writing better ones. I'm sure you can. In fact, why don't you get a pad and pen and for each example I give here, write a little one of your own? I usually find that my students are much better writers than I am.

Action

One of the most frequent mistakes that writers make when they start out is to think of their life stories in terms of information.

Of course, you want to inform the reader about your life and possibly even your views and opinions, but what you don't want to do is to turn your story into a list of dull facts.

49

A life story that reads like a bus time-table or a telephone directory will soon have the reader moving on, looking for a more satisfying read.

The problem lies, strangely enough, in the fact that, as writers, we are dealing with words. Our natural inclination is to think in terms of words. Whereas, what we should really be doing is thinking in terms of images, then looking for the words to match them.

Simply banging out an endless stream is not enough. The reader loses patience and is not gripped. We, the writers, need to be able to make our readers "see" the word picture that we have set out in front of them.

You will often hear the instruction "show, don't tell" used in this context. "Show, don't tell" is the writer's mantra. Usually, it is much better to *show* your readers something than it is to *tell* them.

Let me explain. Suppose you want to describe a person you once met. This person is called Arthur. He is a bookkeeper. He is very nervous and has black hair.

You could write:

Arthur was a bookkeeper. He had black hair and was very nervous.

Frankly, it's a bit dull to read. You are *telling* your readers about Arthur.

On the other hand, you can make it a little more interesting, by *showing* your readers this information. You might write something like:

Arthur looked up from his accounts and pushed his black hair from his eyes with a trembling hand.

If Arthur is a more important character in your story, you might try something a little bit more complex.

At first sight, Arthur looked composed as he filled out the accounts book. His dark hair even lent him an air of seriousness. If you looked closer, the trembling hands showed that he was even more nervous than we were.

In other words, what we are doing is showing Arthur doing something that in turn shows the reader that he is nervous.

Keep Concrete

Hey, that sounds like an instruction. Or perhaps it's a graffito on a sixties building about to be pulled down. "Keep concrete!"

Let me explain what I mean by "keeping concrete". It's very closely allied to the idea of "show, don't tell".

When we write, it is very easy to end up using abstract vocabulary that doesn't actually show the reader a great deal. We describe someone as "beautiful", we write things like "the view was indescribable" (that one should be a criminal offence), "it was very evocative", "Paris is lovely".

Some people would condemn this as lazy writing. It isn't. It's natural writing. It's when we come to revise our work that it's lazy to have left it in there. Even the greatest of writers are capable of scattering their first drafts with these abstract terms.

If you look through your work and find something like "Granddad was eccentric", mark it up with a highlighter pen. It's a variation of "show, don't tell" if you like. What the reader wants to know is how was he eccentric? Did he bathe in asses' milk? Did he wear geraniums on his head on the Sabbath? Did children run screaming from him when they saw him or did they find him a source of fun?

"Rosalie was a charmer who couldn't be trusted." Well, let the readers work out for themselves that she was a charmer. Write the episode where she burrows her way into your mother's trust, then runs off with the contents of her purse and we'll know that she's a charmer and a wicked one to boot.

"The hills were gorgeous at that time of year." What was gorgeous about them? Were the leaves on the trees changing colour? Was it the effect of sunlight on snow? Was it the dry stone walls and the sheep? What was it that made you stop and look at those hills and say "these hills are gorgeous"?

Description

Usually when we talk about descriptions, we are probably referring to a word-portrait of a person or a place.

I will deal with describing people under the sub-heading "Developing your characters" later in this chapter. For the moment, I want to concentrate on the description of places.

Writing description is one of the skills that most of us were taught in English lessons at school. As a result, we feel fairly confident that we can do it. And we probably can.

The danger with description lies not in the fact that we can do it, but in the fact that it is so easy to overdo it.

A little over 100 years ago, few people had ventured more than a couple of miles from the place they were born. Their visual imagery - their visual vocabulary if you like - was limited to the world that immediately surrounded them. If you worked in an industrial town, chances were you lived there as well. The landscape of your mind would be that of factories, high-density housing and the occasional oasis of green in the middle of a bustling city.

Conversely, the country-dweller might never need leave the valley where he lived and worked. Everything he needed to sustain his everyday existence would be at hand. His food came from the land he worked; his clothes and the tools of his trade were made at home or by local specialist tradesmen and women.

Holidays within the shores of this country were a luxury even for the new, burgeoning middle-classes. Holidays abroad were almost exclusively for the rich. Sailors and soldiers were the most frequent travellers. A journey to India took weeks, not a few hours.

Cheap, fast travel, newspapers and magazines, the cinema, and most importantly of all, television, have changed our horizons, opening up new vistas to us. Each of us now has an encyclopaedic visual vocabulary that three generations ago would have been way beyond the furthest fringes of the imagination of the most prescient and intrepid traveller.

Nowadays, click on your TV set (and you don't even have to travel across the room to do that, because you've got a remote control) and you can be transported almost anywhere. On one channel there is an adventure movie featuring an Alpine ravine. Another channel has a travelogue showing sun-drenched beaches in Bali. Another has a documentary showing us the grimmest Buenos Aires slums.

This increasingly visual understanding of the word around us means that we see the world not in terms of words, but in terms of images. The net effect for you as a writer is that your audience, in general, feels less of a need for long descriptions. It may be fair enough for Thomas Hardy to write seventeen pages showing us the contours of Egdon Heath, but the modern reader has little patience for that. Some might argue it is because our attention spans have been weakened by the evil forces of television; others that we simply don't need the volume of description because somewhere in our memory banks we have pictures that will illustrate a scene for our own purposes. Whatever the reason, we don't need that level of description, because with just a few well-chosen words on the part of the author, we "get the picture".

It is extremely easy to bore your reader with excessive description. It is also very easy for you to get carried away when you are writing description. As great phrase after great phrase tumbles from your pen, you feel it is your bounden duty to record them for your readership. Just remember, that reader may soon lose patience.

Sometimes, less is more.

Let's take that "Alpine Ravine" of a coupe of paragraphs back as an example. I suspect that those two words were all you needed to summon up a picture to your mind.

On the other hand, it is perfectly reasonable to say a little more about it. For instance:

We found ourselves on the edge of a ridge. The mountain fell away below us almost vertically .It was the kind of place where even the most seasoned climber would feel a knot of tension developing in his stomach. In the ravine, the winter snows had already begun to melt revealing the tops of harsh, black rocks, many the size of a small house.

It's worth noting a few of things about this little description.

First, there are people in the scene. In this case it is "we", although the reader, from this tiny snippet, doesn't learn a great deal more about who "we" are. People like to read about people, so adding people into your landscape adds interest for the reader. Perhaps we're going to find out who "we" are later, or maybe we already know.

Second, there is a sense of movement in the piece. All that happens is that we walk to a ridge and look down. However, that means that what we are getting is a moving image of the scene, rather than a still photograph.

Third, there is an emotional tone to the description. In this case, it is something to do with the fear/anxiety/nervousness of looking into a sheer drop.

Put people into your descriptions and have them do things and I guarantee that your writing will be ten times better than using the still camera approach to description.

Atmosphere

Atmosphere is one of those horribly vague words. It's hard to define what we mean by it, but we know when we read something that lacks it: what we're reading just isn't enjoyable.

If you enter an eerie, creepy derelict building, we want to feel your fear and nervousness alongside you. We want to know that your breath hangs in the cold night air, that your legs are trembling, that you feel sick to your stomach. If you don't conjure up a word picture that takes us there, then there is no atmosphere. We want to live your life alongside you.

Similarly, if you are describing a scene from the markets of Marrakech, then we don't just want to know what it looks like. We want to know all about the sounds and the smells. What do the hawkers shout? When you stop for a coffee what does it taste like?

As a writer, you create atmosphere by using a variety of techniques. One of the most common ways of creating atmosphere is by adding sensory description to your writing.

There are, of course, five senses – sight, sound, smell, touch and taste. It would take a truly astounding writer to be able to create atmosphere by appealing to just one of those senses. However, often when we start out as writers, we ignore the fact that we can appeal to five different senses and tend to concentrate on just one – sight.

I'm not going to suggest that every time you write a descriptive passage you include something that appeals to all the senses. In fact, if you do, you'll find it's rather like making a currant cake only to find that all the fruit has globbed together in a lump. It's too rich.

However, if you do write bearing in mind that you want to appeal to more than just the sense of sight, then you will find that your writing is vastly improved for it.

Let me show you what I mean.

Writing using just "sight":

I saw the old man from the corner of my eye. I tried hard not to look at him – with his dirty clothes and matted hair.

We only have "sight" here. We see the dirty clothes and matted hair, but to be honest, we're not getting much, and we're certainly not getting that magic ingredient atmosphere.

So let's try again, using all five senses:

I caught sight of the old man from the corner of my eye. He wore tatty, dirty clothes that reeked like stale cabbage even at twenty paces. As the old man moved towards me, the smell grew stronger, almost overwhelming, until I could feel the first rush of water in my mouth that signalled I was going to be sick. The old man reached out a quivering hand, its fingernails long and blackened with soil and touched my face. His hand was sandpaper on my face – rough, harsh, unforgiving. My heart drummed a tattoo in my chest.

- Sight – the tatty, dirty clothes
- Smell – the reek of stale cabbage
- Taste – the rush of water
- Touch – the sandpapery hand
- Sound – the drumming (also perhaps "touch"?)

You'll see that by cramming in all five senses I've overdone it a bit, but I'm sure you understand what I'm driving at. What we now have is atmosphere. We're now alongside the narrator, wondering what is going to happen to him next.

It's such a simple technique. Bring several of the senses to your writing and you will find that you will quickly draw in that sixth sense – atmosphere.

Developing characters

There are several traps that are easy to fall into when we are talking about the characters in our story.

The main one, especially for anyone new to writing, is to think that the reader needs to know absolutely everything that you know about the person you are writing about.

As a rule of thumb, the reader doesn't need to know everything. After all, you don't know everything about that person. Let's face it, it's impossible to know everything that there is to know about anybody. We don't even know ourselves totally. We don't know what other people think about us and as we forget large chunks of what we have done; we're an incomplete portrait even in our own heads.

So, your reader really doesn't need to know everything. You, the writer, have to decide how much the reader needs to know. "How much is that?" you ask. Well, frankly, there's no good answer. However, common sense would dictate that if your granny is only a passing character in your story, we probably need to know a lot less about her than we do about your father, who is one of the pivotal characters in your tale. And do we really need to know your father's shoe size, unless of course he was a size sixteen, in which case that's pretty interesting.

It's also a common beginners' mistake to give us a wodge of information about a new character the moment that character is introduced.

Harder to do, much more satisfying both for the reader, and for your sense of achievement as a writer, is to drip feed the information that we need about a character into the course of your story.

Another common mistake, is to describe our characters "statically". By that, I mean that we paint a word picture of what that person is like, but it is like a still photograph, like the kind of description of places we were trying to avoid just a few pages ago.

Writing about one of the characters in your life as they go about some task is far more rewarding. That task doesn't have to be anything particularly esoteric, either. I have read brilliant character descriptions of grannies baking, younger brothers assembling and disassembling mopeds in the kitchen sink, fathers putting up rickety shelving and sisters getting ready for a night out. It's not always in the big events of life that we reveal our characters to the world.

For example, if your mother was a stickler for neatness and cleanliness, you might write something like this:

Mother had spent the first decade of married life in army quarters. Every time they moved house, which was often, they would be subjected to the "white glove inspection" of their army-provided housing.

Some junior officer or NCO, with little to keep him busy in a peacetime army, would be dispatched to the house to inspect every wall, surface and ceiling for the slightest sign of dilapidation. Anything wrong and the cost was deducted from Dad's pay.

Paintwork must be scratch free, windows diamond-bright, skirting-boards must show not the slightest mark of a clumsy, passing boot. Finally, the inspector would snap on a pair of virginal white cotton gloves and run a suspicious finger over fixtures and fittings. Dust was the final enemy.

As a result, mother had adopted a military routine to tidying and cleaning the house. Feather duster tucked like a swagger-stick under one arm, she marshalled abandoned dinky toys, lonely slippers and building blocks into serried ranks on the kitchen table.

Bobby pins and Kirkby grips, Action Man's leg or stray bubble-gum cards of Mickey Dolenz would be squadroned according to whom she had decided was their owner. And, oh, the humiliation of being the one with the most articles on that table.

Next came the blitzkrieg on the sitting-room. Dad's easy-chair was body-searched for stray change that might have fallen down the loose covers tucked into its sides and back.

Spiders were driven from their homelands, their cobwebs razed as Mother swept away all that lay before her. Like the cavalry, mother showed no quarter.

But, despite the military precision of her cleaning, there was always the cigarette, jammed and jiggling at the corner of her mouth.

When writing about the people in your story, you may find it useful to jot down a few notes about that person. Here is a list of the kinds of things you might note.

- Name, including nicknames or family names
  Age or age span during the course of your book, or at the time of the events you are describing
  Date of birth – what else happened that year? Place of birth – what's the place like?
- Height
- Weight
- Colour of hair
- Colour of eyes
- Habits
- Mannerisms
- Scars & distinguishing features – how did they get them?
- Handicaps – e.g. where did the limp come from?
- Way of speaking – e.g. Gentle and slow? Sharp and with a strong local accent? Precisely?
- Job(s)

- Brothers & sisters
- Place in family (e.g. eldest child)
- Kind of house they live(d) in
- Education
- Ambitions
- Friends
- Weaknesses
- Skills
- Interests
- Favourite colour
- Favourite food
- What other information do you want us to know about this person?

You are unlikely to pass on all this information to the reader. If you told your readers all this in the space of a few paragraphs, they would be overwhelmed with information. However, it's the kind of note taking that will help you to focus on the person about whom you are writing.

Openings

How often have you opened a book in a bookshop or library, read the first few lines and either been hooked or turned off by what you read? I imagine there must be some people who will read anything, regardless of how awful those first few lines are, but most of us, I suspect, need to have our attention gripped from the start.

The beginning is the most important part of your story. It is vital that you write it well, so that your reader will carry on reading. A good opening doesn't have to be clever-clever, but it should intrigue us, hook us into the writer's world and make us read onto the next line and then the next and so on. So, in essence, a good opening:

- interests the reader enough to make him or her read on

- establishes the tone and mood of the piece you are writing. Is it serious or comic, conversational or literary or one for the book group?
- sets up a 2-way relationship between reader and writer
- gives some kind of indication of what the subject matter is going to be and how the writer is going to deal with that subject matter

There are as many ways to write openings as there are to write anything. However several common ways of writing them are:

- a simple declarative statement – "I've loved horses since I could first say the word."
- dialogue – " 'You, my boy, are the laziest, rudest, messiest child that it has ever been my misfortune to teach,' said Mr. Shepherd."
- a surprising statement – "I'm the only person in our family who's still got their appendix."

Make your reader ask themselves questions. Who is this person? Why are they doing that? Who's with them? Who are they talking to? Isn't that dangerous?

Intrigue them a little and they are much more likely to carry on reading. Bear in mind that you, the writer, are the only person who knows what happens next in your story. The reader has to read on to find out what it is you are going to say.

Dialogue

I don't know if you've ever read an autobiography and thought "how can they remember exactly what so-and-so said to them? That was fifty years ago!" The truth is that they didn't remember exactly. They reconstructed the event, writing dialogue of their own.

You may be able to remember one or two things verbatim - the time your teacher picked on you for no apparent reason or the time your boss told you you were the best thing since sliced bread. But, in reality, most of us have fuzzy memories about what people have said to us over the years.

You are allowed a little licence. If you write a life story with no dialogue in it at all, then it will be very stodgy indeed. In fact, it will probably be unreadable.

Take the following:

Mother wanted me to get a job in an office, but I wanted to work outdoors. We argued about it, until eventually she let me go and work on Thompson's farm, where I knew there was a job going.

What an opportunity missed! This is an ideal place in your story for some dialogue.

"I've seen Bob Cox and he says there's a job going as a junior at Hetherington's"

"I'm not going to Hetherington's."

"It's a good job. He says if you do well, then in a few months time you can get day release."

"Wow. You mean they'll let me out of the office one day a week?"

"Don't take that tone with me. It's got prospects. Play your cards right and they'll teach you to type."

"I don't want to learn how to type."

"But typing's the future. In five or six years, you could even be a secretary."

"I'm not working cooped up in an office all day."

Even just as bare dialogue, this works much better than the original. I have deliberately left out the "he said/she said" to make the point. In fact, I could probably get away with that in this context, because there are only two people speaking and it's fairly obvious who is saying what. However, if the dialogue went on any longer, it would be worth popping in the odd "said Mother/said I" just to remind the reader of who's speaking.

The worst kind of dialogue is often referred to as "ping-pong" dialogue. That's because one person serves up a question and the other person simply replies.

"I understand you're not happy at work."
"That's true."
"Is it your boss?"
"Yes."
"What is it about him?"
"He expects me to do too much."
"What kinds of things does he expect you to do?"
"Oh, work late, do unpaid overtime, that kind of thing."

This is fine if one of your characters is trying to wheedle some information out of another, but if all your dialogue ends up sounding like a lawyer's cross-examination, then you're not going to grab the reader.

You have to make your dialogue sound like people talking. This is easier to say than it is to do.

Make what they say too stilted and grammatical – and it won't sound like speech. It'll sound like some kind of textbook.

On the other hand, if you were to copy the exact way in which people talk, it would be too much. Every time we speak, we are a mass of hesitations and speech tics. We start a sentence seeming to be talking about one thing, change our minds part way through and end up talking about something else. Most annoyingly of all, when we speak, we don't do punctuation.

You also need to make a decision about local accents and dialect. There's no hard and fast rule on this one, but unless your book is going to have a very limited local appeal, it's probably best to cut dialect as such to a minimum.

However, there are some aspects of speech that can be found in all sorts of different dialects. Words such as "gotta", "wanna" or "cos", for "got to", "want to" and "because" are commonly used. Many people, when they speak, lose the ends of words – "doin'" for "doing", or fail to aspirate the "h", "'ouse" for "house".

There is no reason why you can't use a sprinkling of these words to show that a character is speaking in dialect, but be careful. Whilst we may understand these words easily when they are spoken, they're sometimes very hard to follow when written on the page.

If you want to indicate a strong regional accent, you can always write " 'I'm not doing it, and that's that,' he said in his strong Yorkshire accent" or something similar. The advantage of this is that the reader can "do" their own Yorkshire accent in their head, and whilst you may be able to tell Hull from Bradford, Leeds from the Dales, it actually doesn't matter to the reader. The accent in the reader's head is good enough, even if it's nearer rural Lancashire or, for that matter, Gloucestershire than the Yorkshire dialect you were writing.

A further way of indicating dialect is by the use of grammar that is typical of speech rather than the written word. In order to be grammatically correct, we might write "He was sitting on a chair". However, your character might say "He was sat on a chair."

Being aware that there is a difference between spoken grammar and written grammar is important not only in relation to dialect, but also needs to be borne in mind when writing any kind of dialogue. People speak differently to the way in which language is written.

If you have to use words that are specifically local, you can either explain them in the text or even use an asterisk and give a "translation" in the footer of the page. If you are using an extensive number of local or specialised words, then it might even be worthwhile putting together a short glossary. My inclination would be to have this somewhere at the front of the book, rather than at the back, so that the reader spots it before he or she gets into the main body of your work.

Some people find dialogue really difficult to write. If you are one of these people, try the following little exercise.

Take an episode from your life that involved you and one other person. An argument, an interview or some kind of confrontation often works well for this.

Write the episode purely in dialogue – almost like the script for a radio play. Afterwards, add in the narrative to flesh the story out.

The result may not be perfect, but as with any skill, you need to practise it to get results.

The Flashback

This is a really useful device that you will be familiar with from films and books.

It is very easy to start at the beginning, with your birth, and simply carry on writing until you catch up with yourself. There is nothing wrong with this, but if you can shift a little from one time to another, it makes your story all the more interesting. It gives your story a context.

Certainly, using the difference between our modern, generally more pampered lives and the harshness of our world a generation or two ago, is a good way to start a flashback.

Another great advantage of the flashback is that you can start with something happening. Once you use a flashback, you are then able to flesh in details of events that occur before your story starts – what we call "back story".

We are now aware that each episode of your story needs to start with some kind of action. We've also already seen that if we introduce each new character with a welter of information, it can get rather boring. One way around this is to introduce a character by having them do something – then by filling in something of the character's background later.

"There you go," said Arthur, lifting an unfeasibly large parcel off his bicycle," I'll just check the list with you."

Arthur pulled out the list and began ticking off the items as we put them on the kitchen table.

"One tin of baked beans, catering size... check ... One melon, honeydew ... check ..."

Arthur had been in the RAF. He ran through the routine of delivering groceries as though he were preparing a Lancaster Bomber for a night-time raid. There were some in the village who suggested that the nearest he'd ever been to an aeroplane was Farnborough Air Show, but .....

The technique of "back story" works equally well for descriptions of places.

We arrived shortly after midnight. The key was where it always was and we let ourselves in, swiftly lit both fire and stove and began dragging in luggage and groceries from the car.

We'd rented this cottage for the past five years and each year we'd grown to know and love its idiosyncrasies more and more...

In both these examples, which have been kept deliberately short, you will see that we are into the back story after only a sentence or two. In both cases, I could have gone on to write a great deal more before turning back to fill in the details that I feel the reader wants to know, but this is a short book and I'm sure you've grasped the idea.

Conflict

A story is not a story without some kind of conflict. Without conflict, what you write will be a bloodless, lifeless limp rag of an essay that no one will want to read. When writers refer to conflict, they don't necessarily mean conflict in the largest sense of the word. Conflict can, of course, mean warfare, fighting or blazing rows, but in literary terms it includes much smaller ideas. Differences between people in your story can give rise to conflict, without resorting to bloodshed. For instance:

- Your desire to get to University despite a background where you are expected to go out to work at fifteen is an example of conflict.
- You wanted to escape the city life and go and live in the country. Your wife didn't. It didn't end in divorce, but it's still conflict.
- You fancy a sun-drenched holiday on a Caribbean island, surrounded by hot and cold running waiters; your husband wants to pitch a tent in the Cairngorms. That's conflict.

There is also a type of conflict that we refer to as "inner conflict".

- Should I have said what I said?
- What did it take for me to go up in an aeroplane when I was scared stiff of flying?
- Should I have had the last potato when Freda only had three?

Writing conflict is not a technique in itself. When you write conflict, you need to bring to bear some of the other ideas in this chapter – description, dialogue, flashbacks, atmosphere. Writing conflict is an attitude of mind.

You might argue that conflict is the territory of the fiction writer. True, but this book is, in part at least, about how the techniques of the fiction writer can improve your life story writing. You might also argue that there are some superb memoirs of idyllic lives where little seems to go wrong. True, but if you examine these stories in detail, you will soon see that all is not as smooth as it might at first look. Things go wrong even in the most perfect of settings:

- The car breaks down on the way to your holiday destination.
- Your mother buys an expensive dress that she then decides she doesn't like and has to hide it from your father, who is on an economy drive.
- The teacher punishes you for flicking an ink pellet, when in fact it was Keith Thomas in the next desk.

Even in the calmest seas of life, there are days when it gets a little choppy. Choppy seas are far more interesting than flat ponds. Now storm-whipped oceans ...

Tension and Pace

The sister skill of using conflict is understanding how to use tension and pace to build up your story.

The simplest way to alter the pace of your story is to alter sentence length. If the action is frantic, we want short, sharp sentences. If the sun is shining and you're sipping iced gin and tonic with not a care in the world, then we expect a longer, more measured sentence. However, don't forget that the length of your paragraphs is at least as important as sentence length. Take a look at any book and you'll see the difference between a long descriptive paragraph and some short, sharp exchanges of dialogue without having to read the work. You can see it in what we call the "white space".

Here are some handy tips on pace:

- If you are writing scenes involving action, make the sentences short.
- Vary the length of your sentences to give the reader changes in pace.
- Use good, strong verbs, rather than pairing up a weak verb with an adverb. For instance, if someone "walked slowly", what exactly are they doing? Could you replace "walked slowly" with "ambled", or "shambled" or "staggered" or "limped" or "sauntered"?

Check for the number of adjectives you have used. We all tend to over-use adjectives and slip in too many. Instead of painting a word-picture, you can quickly bog down your story. Read your work out loud. Is it easy to read, or do you find yourself stumbling over awkward phrases? If you do, then the reader will as well. Your story will lack pace.

There are other ways to change the pace of your story.

It's worth thinking about these in cinematic terms. At the end of a film scene, there are several ways in which we can move onto the next scene. Sometimes the camera lingers as the hero drives into the distance. Sometimes we cut to something unconnected – a flock of birds flying overhead. Sometimes we leap forward ten years in time with an appropriate sub-title to show us where we are. At other times, there is a slow dissolve as the hypnosis takes effect on the prisoner's mind and we know that we are going to regress to his childhood.

Moving from one scene to the next is an important business. Sometimes, you may be tempted to link two episodes some time apart by writing several paragraphs, perhaps even a chapter. When you read it, you think to yourself "This really is boring." But how else are you going to cover the ground?

Think film. What's wrong with simply jumping ahead ten years?

Ten years later, I found myself in exactly the same predicament....

It gets your story to where you want it to be and the reader hasn't dozed off during your paragraph (or even chapter) of stodgy filler. There are other times when you can use a kind of "jump cut" to great effect.

Let us suppose that you are going to write that scene when you and your husband are disagreeing over a holiday destination.

Your husband arrives back from work to find you up to your armpits in brochures marked "Caribbean Paradise" and "Beat the winter blues and fly somewhere warm".

Under his arm, he has three skinny rolls. They turn out to be a two-man bivouac the size of a child's play-tent, which when fully erected gives you headroom of seventeen inches and two bed rolls. He expects to you to put one of these between you and the ground. It's the thickness of a five-pence piece.

You argue for warmth and sunshine. He argues for adventure and hardiness.

Your parting shot to him is "I'm not going camping in the Cairngorms and that's final."

Of course, for the sake of our story, you do end up camping in the Cairngorms. If this is a film, what's the best scene to show next?

We could see your husband packing equipment, you both getting into the car, driving to the Cairngorms, pitching the tent, slowly beginning to get colder and colder.

Or, we cut straight to a picture of you shivering in a tent in sub-zero temperatures, slapping mittened hands round your blanketed body.

Obviously, the second way of moving the story to the Cairngorms is vastly superior. It is snappier, wittier and will have a far greater impact on your audience.

But pace isn't always about speeding up your story. Sometimes you need to slow it down.

Again, a frequent habit of beginning writers is to write their stories in too skeletal a form. In an effort to get the facts down, they forget that someone else is going to read their work. If you put the ideas and techniques from this chapter into practice, you'll soon find that your writing becomes more fleshed out. What you write will no longer be the blanched skeleton of your life, but something of flesh and blood – a living story of your life story.

Titles

Lastly, a few words about titles.

I always have tremendous difficulty thinking of titles for anything I write. In fact, I have a suspicion that at least half of all the writing I've ever had published has had its title changed. So, I have to confess that this section is the work of a hypocrite.

It's up to you whether or not you want a title for each segment, section or chapter of your book (depending on how it's divided). If you do then you're actually creating quite a lot of work for yourself.

In fact, you may not feel that you need any kind of title at all other than "Marmaduke Trembath – My Life" or "Gloria Gusset – Fifty Years in Knitwear". However, unless you're particularly famous, in which case someone is probably ghost-writing your story anyway, then this kind of title is best used only if you're planning on handing out a few copies round friends and family.

Finding a good title is like panning for gold. If you haven't got a title for your story when you begin, don't panic. You will think of something eventually. You need to keep that notebook handy for the moment inspiration strikes. And it could strike anywhere. "Who's Afraid of Virginia Wolf" is supposedly a piece of graffiti that Edward Albee saw on a lavatory wall.

You can try jotting down a few ideas. What are the main themes of your book? Is there one part that seems to sum up your life?

You can always rely on the journalist's stock title-making mechanisms. These include:

•   Finding an apt quotation. Dozens of books, films and plays use snippets of Shakespeare and other classics for their titles.

•   Using a well-known phrase or saying, then giving it a twist. "The email of the species is more deadly than the mail" is one title I used for an article about the Internet. It's a brilliant title, though I confess I stole it, but I'm not going to say from whom.

•   Telling the public what they're going to get. "A life in the Yorkshire Dales", but be careful here. You can end up sounding a bit like poor old Gloria Gusset.

•   Extracting little phrases that you particularly like from your writing.

Finally, although there is no copyright on titles, there's actually little point in using a well-known title. "Wuthering Heights" by Arthur Johnson or "The Lord of the Rings" by Cynthia Harbottle are not going to fly off the shelves.

So, now you've written your life story in scintillating prose that has atmosphere, tension, pace, coruscating dialogue and an opening that will pin your reader to the floor, what are you going to do next?

Well, I've got some bad news for you. You're about to start rewriting it all. It's a tough old world, so let me show you how ...

Chapter 5 - Re-writing, Revising and Editing Your Work

....

"Whatever sentence will bear to be read twice, we may be sure was thought twice." Henry David Thoreau

In the last few chapters, we've looked at the creative side of writing. I hope that I've given you the confidence to write as well as you can.

In Chapter 3, I wrote about encouraging Writing Brain to take over whilst you are in writing mode. This is a great way of covering the page (or the screen) as quickly as is humanly possible. However, unless you are an absolute genius it is unlikely that you can spill several hundred words onto the page without having to revise them in some way.

Yes, there are days when we write freely and our words flow easily. Often on these days, we need to make only the slightest of changes to what we've written. But we do need to make changes. On other days, the words that dribble out will form a dollopy porridge that needs complete revision, or possibly even complete eradication.

Looking at what you have written, and re-writing where you think it is necessary, is what separates the poor amateur writer from the accomplished professional. It really is as straightforward as that. As the playwright Sheridan once wrote "easy writing's cursed hard reading". Sentences that flow smoothly when you read the final version may have started out as clumsy, awkward clumps of words. The professional writer takes these infelicities and moulds and shapes them into something smooth and easy to read.

We're about to do the same thing with your manuscript. Now that we've accomplished our task of getting our story down on paper comes the hard part of re-working it to make it the best we can possibly accomplish. Now, we've got to bring that Editorial Brain to the forefront.

Editorial Brain is the critical, analytical side of the brain. You need this little chap if you are going to sharpen up what you've written and make your reader want to read on.

Don't think that the process of rewriting, revising and editing your work needs to be a dull slog. For some people, the process of re-writing is much more enjoyable than the writing itself. Some writers prefer the languid pace of honing, polishing and re-shaping to the hard graft of actually getting words down onto that blank piece of paper.

However, if you are new to writing, you might find this the hardest part. Suddenly, instead of adding words to the page, you're subtracting them. You find yourself crossing out whole paragraphs that took ages to write. Everything you have written goes under the microscope and you have to become your own stern critic. Sometimes it feels a little like you have been building your own house for months on end and you have to demolish the whole of a gable end to put something right.

Types of Revision

One of the problems we have when we talk about revising or editing your work is that this can mean anything from removing an entire chapter (or even more), to inserting or deleting a comma.

Some authors of how-to-write books suggest a fixed number of times that you revise a work. Some also suggest that you wait until you have finished all your writing before you start revising.

As you can tell, I'm not a great one for trying to lay down golden rules as to how something should or should not be done. You will by now have developed a whole range of strategies for getting your writing done; you will in turn also develop your own methods and approaches for revising your work.

As revision/editing can mean so many different things, let's look at what that implies for you as an author.

Big Revision

At the mega-level, before you start getting down to the nitty-gritty, I think it is worth reading your finished manuscript all the way through. If you do this the minute you've typed the last full stop on the last page, you may find that you are too close to what you have written to be objective in your opinions.

Many writers like to put a manuscript away in a desk drawer for a few weeks, even months, before coming back to it. This gives them a chance to read the work almost as though it were written by someone else.

However, let's be realistic about this. Leaving your freshly-printed manuscript to one side for three months is a tough demand. After all, you've just finished writing it, you want to get on with the job of tarting it up ready for someone else to read it. You'll probably be hankering to fiddle with it as soon as you can.

If you can leave it to lie fallow for a few weeks, I think you will find that it will do you a power of good. It will give both mind and body time to recuperate from the hard slog and your words will seem so much fresher to you.

On the other hand, there are many writers who start each day's writing session by re-reading what they wrote the previous day, making revisions and alterations where they see fit and using this almost like a warm-up exercise for the writing session ahead.

There are a couple of problems with this kind of revision.

First, you are revising at a micro-level. Imagine that yesterday you wrote an episode of 1500 words about the time you were caught stealing chewing gum from the corner shop (shame on you!). You will be able to alter all sorts of things in the piece – grammar, spelling, punctuation, cheesy phrases, bits where you've tried too hard to sound like a real writer. What you won't be able to sense is if that episode fits into the overall pattern of your book.

Second, you can get caught up in the process of revision and spend hours fiddling with a sentence, writing it one way then another, whereas what you really need to be doing is getting words down onto paper.

A sensible compromise might be to start each day with a little light re-writing, just to get warmed up, but not to get caught-up in-depth.

Don't worry if you end up cutting a whole episode or even a chapter or more. It may seem entirely painful at first. In fact, it may be painful to you no matter how often you do it, but even if you never get used to it, you will eventually become resigned to the fact that it has to be done.

Stick with the Big Picture
When you do come to read the first draft of your manuscript, it is tempting to take a red pen to it and flag up every little spelling mistake and clumsy phrase.

In fact, it's almost impossible not to do this. Sometimes you'll wonder if you ever learnt any English at all, when you come across sentences or paragraphs that mean absolutely nothing.

It's difficult, but I think that at this stage you should try to avoid getting too deeply into the minutiae of your manuscript. You need to be reading it from an almost structural point-of-view.

For instance, imagine you have written a 100,000 words manuscript – I know I said we were aiming for 50,000, but you've worked extremely hard. When you come to read the manuscript, you realise that although the book is supposed to be about your whole life, three-quarters of it is in fact about your childhood in India at the end of the Second World War.

You may decide that this makes your book rather unbalanced. You have used 75,000 words to describe ten years of your life and 25,000 words to tell us about the other sixty.

Hard though it is, you need to lose as much as a quarter of the book in order to concentrate purely on that Indian childhood.

Now, don't throw yourself off a cliff if this happens to you. If you simply remove the 25,000 words about your later life, you can keep them in another file on your computer and use it as the start of volume 2!

At this stage in your revision process, you should be asking yourself such questions as:

- Does the book feel balanced?
- Which sections work particularly well?
- Which sections don't work well? Should they be improved, or removed?
- Is there anything I have left out that would improve the structure of the book?

At this stage, you should also be loath to pass on your manuscript for anyone else to read. Most people are used to reading finished, polished works. They probably don't understand what a book looks like and reads like in the early stages of its development.

It's also extremely difficult to know whose opinion is best. If you ask someone whose main literary diet is thrillers to read your gentle story of an idyllic rural childhood – the kind of book they would never read even if it were given it for Christmas – then you are not going to get a balanced reply. Your book is simply not their kind of book – no matter how well (or badly) written it might be.

You even have to be careful of asking your spouse or partner to read it. Spouses and partners are notoriously incapable of giving any rational opinion. Either they will love it simply because it is you who has written it or, and I'm afraid this is all too common, they will simply pick out a few spelling mistakes and some mangled sentences and all your hard work is damned in two minutes of negative opinion.

I can't stress strongly enough that this is probably not a good stage at which to ask someone to read your work. It is still too personal to you, you still have a lot of revision to do and, after all that hard work, it is so easy for you to be knocked back by an unkind word. You might prefer instead to move to the next stage of revision

Revising for energy

We all want our work to have "energy". We want the words to come alive; we want them to rise up off the page.

At some point in the revision process, you need to be looking at your work to see if everything you have written will engage your reader. If it lies flat on the page, it won't.

Writing too much is one of the modern curses. Owning a computer makes it extremely easy to hack words into a machine. Don't worry if you have written too much. In fact, on the contrary, you should be ecstatic, because it gives you far more material to work with. Indeed, cutting things is harder if you only got a few words down in the first place

Imagine you've sat down to write for a couple of hours and have written a thousand words. Later, you're reading over what you've written and you suddenly realise that 800 of them are listless, lifeless and pointless.

If you cut those 800 words, suddenly that writing session becomes an eking out of a couple of hundred words.

It may hurt to get rid of 80% of what you've written, but ask yourself a question. Do you want to be the author of a thousand mediocre words, or to have written a great piece of 200 words?

Ideally, you'd have liked to have produced a cracking piece of a thousand words straight off. Wouldn't we all. Unfortunately, the writing life isn't like that. Hard though it is, your best course of action is to get out your coloured pen and excise the dull bits.

So, whenever you read over a piece you have written, you need to ask yourself the questions:

- is it interesting?
- will this make the reader read on?
- is it exciting/engaging/endearing?
- does it touch on human emotions?

If you feel that what you've written doesn't do these things, then you need to be prepared to cut what you've written.

So far, however, we have concentrated on cutting. There may be other occasions on which what you have written feels too skeletal. You want some flesh on the bones.

For instance, you might have introduced a character who you thought would play a minor role. On re-reading, you find that this character is more important to your story than you had expected. Perhaps the reader needs to know more about this character, more about his/her background. There's nothing wrong with this. Revision isn't simply a process of subtraction. However, be warned. Sometimes, when you introduce new material, it can alter the overall structure of what you are writing. Also, it is very easy to end up padding out your work to fill space. This, of course, flies in the face of what you are trying to do, which is to make what you've written crisp, energetic, and reader-friendly.

Editing for Meaning

If you have been through the processes outlined above, you have done the hardest work of all. Everything from now on in is just a process of "tarting up" your manuscript. It still requires you to have your wits about you, but the big decisions have now been made.

It is very important now to check through your work to make sure that what you have written says what you want it to say.

One of the first things to check is the words you have used. It is very easy to become "writerly" and start using long words. These don't normally impress readers; they put them off. So, it is important to ensure that anyone reading your book can understand what it is you are trying to tell them.

If, for instance, you are hoping to sell your book "Thirty years in the Nuclear Industry" to the general public, then you need to make sure that the book is written at a level that the general public will understand. A book filled with the jargon of the nuclear industry will probably only sell to anyone who knows you and a handful of physicists.

One of the most frequent mistakes made by new writers is that their sentences are too long. Now, this doesn't mean that you have to insult the reader by making every sentence six words long. However, you need to bear in mind that long, complex sentences will put off the vast majority of readers. Even people who have the most highly developed reading habits do not want to wade through sentences that spill out for fifty-plus words.

Editing for spelling, grammar and punctuation

As soon as you mention spelling, grammar and punctuation, out come the hawks. Whenever I teach this aspect of writing, somehow my classes dissolve into debates on the state of education in schools.

The pendulum swings in every walk of life. In children's education we have gone from an educational system where accuracy was far more important than originality, through days when "creativity" and "free thought" were more important than clarity, to the modern system where children of 6 can explain the difference between a gerund and a gerundive.

Often with my classes, I meet the two extreme results of the British system. I have students who are terrified of setting a word on paper for fear of putting a comma in the wrong place. They find themselves sitting alongside students who will produce, at the drop of a hat, reams of material that defies all known grammar systems.

Let me state clearly that I think that spelling, grammar and punctuation are extremely important. I hate it when I misspell anything and when I come across one of my sentences in which I have mangled the English language beyond tolerable belief, I cringe. I can't make up my mind whether the apostrophe should be banned, or if I should equip myself with a fat red pen and run riot amongst the market stalls of Britain.

The concept of "correct" English is extremely hard to pin down. Language is constantly changing and evolving. There are aspects of those changes that can be very annoying. I find "prevaricate", which means to tell a lie, used instead of procrastinate particularly annoying. I also get wound-up by "aggravating" for "irritating", "momentarily", when used for "in a moment" and "infer" misused for "imply".

Those are some of my bugbears; I'm sure you have some of your own. However, try not to get too hot under the collar about "correct" usage, but strive to be clear and precise in what you write.

Whilst I can swing from pedant to profligate in the same sentence, I still believe you can get too hung up on these issues whilst you are actually in the process of writing your book. It can stop you from making progress. If you are too worried that your English is "correct", then it can mean that the end result of your work, even after much revising, is stilted and stuffy.

Whilst spelling is not a matter of personal choice – most words have one or perhaps two spellings, punctuation and grammar are more slippery eels.

If you have tried to write in such a way as to make your story conversational, it is sometimes hard to apply the strictest of grammar rules. Normally, for instance, a sentence needs a verb – a doing word – to be a sentence. However, you can write sentences without verbs. Like this one. Dickens did.

But it should be stressed that you still can't ignore all the reasonable demands of grammar if your readers are to make head or tail of your work.

If you find grammar, and for that matter punctuation, difficult, perhaps you weren't taught these things at school. Get down to your local bookshop and buy yourself a book on the subject.

I would, however, like to make one point about punctuation. You may find that your sentences tend to be longer than they need. One useful trick to shorten them is to replace some of the commas you have used with a full stop. This won't work every time, but will help. Similarly, check for "ands" and "buts". There's nothing wrong in using these, but you may find that you have linked two very long clauses that would read better if separated by a full stop.

The kind of editing where you are looking for spelling, grammar and punctuation mistakes is often referred to as "proof reading". It is the very last stage of any editing process. Some people might see it as nit picking. I think this is a mistake. Publishers allow for the fact that their authors are human (I typed that as "there authors", incidentally and didn't spot it straight away). They don't mind the occasional mistake. However, a manuscript that is full of misspellings, bad punctuation and mangled grammar is not going to improve your chances of publishing success.

Don't rely on your spell-checker, either. Spell-checkers are extremely useful tools for spotting when you have written "usfeul" instead of "useful". However, if like me, your fingers are awkward, lumpen and don't ever seem to hit the keys in the order in which your brain is sending out signals, then you will end up with plenty of words that are misspelled, but that are perfectly valid words in their own right. For instance, I am forever typing "form" instead of "from" and vice versa. We all know the difference between "two", "to" and "too", but it is very easy to type in the wrong one whilst your brain is racing.

I would also stress that I think that, no matter how "good" your spelling, punctuation and so forth, it is extraordinarily difficult to pick up your own mistakes. Your eye will tend to see what it expects to see on the page; this can lead to its playing tricks on you.

It is at this stage in the editing process, that you could call on someone else to take a look at your manuscript. You need someone who has a good standard of English, but not someone who is too pedantic. I recently got picked up on my spelling of the word "fogy" and was told that I had misspelled it. It should be "fogey". In fact, my dictionary allows for both spellings. Provided you bribe your proofreading friend with enough drink, they should check things like that out for you.

So, to sum up, don't confuse re-writing your work with tidying up the spelling and grammar. They are separate issues.

Well, if you've stayed with me so far, you've now got a pretty decent idea of what you're doing. In the next chapter, however, I'm going to look at some of the potential dangers of life story writing. Hey ho, it never rains but it pours.

Chapter 6 - Pitfalls for the Life Story Writer

....

"Your manuscript is both good and original; but the part that is good is not original and the part that is original is not good." Dr. Samuel Johnson to a would-be author (identity unknown).

In the last chapter, I tried to concentrate on positive ways of making your writing as good as you can. In this chapter, I'm going to look at some of the negatives and how to put them right.

Before I do, I'd like to re-iterate the advice I gave in Chapter 3 about Writing Brain and Editorial Brain. I still think that for most people the best way to write is to get something down on paper, then play around with it. If you are too critical before you start, you'll never get anything written at all. So, bearing this in mind, here are some thoughts on some of the common traps it's easy to fall into, along with a few ideas of how to remedy them.

Carmen Miranda Syndrome

As you're writing about yourself, you may find that you end up using the word "I" a lot. In fact, it's inevitable.

The trouble is with using "I" is that it can exaggerate the effect of everything in your book. So, when you are quite reasonably having a minor crow about a success, it can turn you into a vainglorious, boasting egotist. Similarly, if you are describing troubled times, it can make you sound like a whingeing, whining defeatist.

There are some straightforward ways to reduce the I-I-I effect.

The most useful rule-of-thumb is to avoid starting sentences and especially paragraphs with the word "I".

"I went inside as the door was already open." can easily be re-written. "As the door was already open, I went inside." For some reason, placing the "I" mid-sentence stops it being as intrusive.

Check your sentence openings, and especially your paragraph openings, to see if you have used "I" too much. If you have, think of ways to change the word order to take the emphasis away from the "I".

If your story can take it, why not talk to the reader from time to time? Perhaps use this chat with the reader as a way of moving into a new phase of the story. For instance, perhaps you're writing about how your memory fails you from time to time. You could write something like this:

> *We've all had them. You know what I'm talking about. The fridge moments. We're looking for the boot polish, the radio, the cat and we're standing, staring at the inside of the fridge wondering how on earth we ever got there.*
>
> *Well, things have moved beyond the fridge moment.*
>
> *I don't know if this has ever happened to you. You're walking down the street and you see someone. You know that person. You know them well. You've known them for years You know where they live, how many children they have, what their husband has for lunch on Thursdays. You know everything it's decently possible to know about them, except for the life of you, you can't remember their name.*
>
> *That's exactly what happened to me in July of that year.*

As well as avoiding the over-use of "I", this technique also draws the reader into the story. Bringing the reader into a shared experience helps to overcome the "egotism" of a life story.

Shifting the camera onto different people in your story also means that you stop using "I" too much.

Reginald Bowler came into my life on the 13ᵗʰ March 1953. "Working for me, son, is like being part of a marriage." He forgot to add that it was a marriage made in hell. Each day, as I totted up the columns of pounds, shillings and pence, Reg would sit behind a mound of papers, alternately sucking his tea and his teeth. Occasionally, he would unwind a paperclip and chase stray bits of meat around what remained of his molars.

By placing the camera on Reg, we have now moved our focus onto a description of him. We can write about Reg now and the emphasis is no longer on us. The occasional stray "I" will hardly be noticeable as we will be concentrating on the appalling Reginald Bowler.

Telling us too much about yourself

One of the major decisions you need to make when writing any kind of autobiography is how much you want the reader to know about you. I know this may seem an odd thing to say – after all, you're writing an autobiography. But at one extreme of autobiographical writing is the hugely confessional writing that tells us everything about you and your family and everyone you've ever met.

This kind of writing has its a function. It is often referred to as "writing out the demons". Sometimes things happen in our lives that are so awful that we look for ways in which we can come to terms with them. Writing about these events is one way of doing this.

I'm not convinced that this kind of writing is for anything more than personal consumption, however. Whilst it might do you a power of good to get the matter off your chest, it doesn't always do the reader a power of good having to wade through what you have written. What was catharsis to you may well look like self-indulgence to the reader.

Sometimes, this self-indulgent writing is little more than moaning and whingeing.

Imagine your book as a guest at a dinner party. That guest spends all dinner party whinging on about how hard their life has been and how unfair it all is. Whilst you might be able to lend a sympathetic ear for a few minutes, after a while, you feel like you've been made to sit next to a rain cloud. Everyone else round the table seems to be having witty, animated sunny conversations, but you've been lumped next to someone who's been paid by the Samaritans to drum up custom.

You may not have meant what you write to sound like a whinge, but when you read it back, it sounds like one long rant about how unfair life has been to you. Frankly, who wants to know? If your whole tone is depressive and self-pitying, then nobody in their right mind is going to get further than a couple of pages before giving up.

"Aha," you reply, "but my life has been hard. I've had a lot of unlucky breaks." I'm not for one moment trying to belittle anyone who has had a tough time. If you've had unlucky breaks, write about them with wit and passion. Or else, write about them in a whingeing and moaning fashion, then burn your manuscript. You've got it off your chest now.

Even at a more restrained level, you will have to make some decisions as to what to leave in and take out of your work. If you include the incident when Aunty Doris got drunk at Aunty Flo's funeral and sang the Marsellaise whilst wearing a tea cosy, what repercussions might this have? Will Aunty Doris's children take umbrage? Will others think it sacrilegious to the memory of Saintly Aunty Flo?

You'd be surprised how many toes you could tread on in even the most straightforward of tales, without breaking the law of libel (I will deal with the matter of libel later in this chapter). However, do be warned that some members of your family might see Aunty Doris's behaviour as belonging to that bank of family secrets that shouldn't be paraded in public. Similarly, you might well think that the most interesting people you can write about are your family's black sheep – and yes, you're right, they're far more interesting than the law-abiding, morally incorruptible ones with steady jobs Others might see any re-telling of tales about these black sheep as bringing shame on the family.

If in doubt, get someone whose opinion you trust to cast an eye over any sections of your writing that you think might cause upset. You might find that just by toning down one or two aspects of the story, you can tell it without offence yet still make it a good read.

Regional and Specialist Matters

We've already dealt with regional dialect and accent in the last chapter. All regions also have their own vocabularies. An alley in one part of the country becomes a lonning in another and a ginnel in yet another.

Similarly, all trades and professions have their own vocabularies. For anyone who does not know either an area of the country or the language of a particular trade, using jargon or dialect words can be off-putting if they are not used with care.

I think that there are three main ways of dealing with this.

The first is to give a direct explanation.

> *Arthur had brought his bait box with him. A bait box (unsurprisingly enough) contained your "bait", in other words your mid-morning snack or lunch.*

The second is to make it obvious from the context.

> *Every time I went into the ginnel I felt nervous. It was dark and damp along there, and there was hardly room even for a six-year old to stretch out his arms. If you did, you could feel the walls of the back yards on either side of you, walls that rose up tall above your head, making the space seem even more enclosed.*

The third is quite simply to provide a glossary of terms as suggested previously.

Writing Economically – Sticking to the Point

A frequent beginner's mistake is to give us far more detail than we really want to know. We've all come across this sort of story:

> *I was sipping my cup of tea and watching the ten o'clock news, when suddenly there was a ring at the door.*
>
> *"Who could that be at ten o'clock in the evening?" I asked myself.*
>
> *I got up from the armchair, crossed the room and went down the hall to the front door, which I had carefully locked at around 7.30 that very evening.*
>
> *"Hi, Carole." It was David. "I hope it's not too late. I know it's ten o'clock, but I saw the lights were on."*

Not only is this tedious, but we're not sure what information is important. From this, in fact, it would seem that the fact that it is 10 o'clock is the most important aspect of the piece. After all, the writer has managed to mention the fact three times in the space of a handful of sentences.

Let's assume that the following information is relevant:

- Carole is relaxing
- It's 10 o'clock at night
- David is apologetic about calling round so late

What's wrong with:

> *One evening, I was relaxing in front of the 10 o'clock news, when the doorbell rang.*
>
> *A hugely apologetic David greeted me.*

The second piece is less than one third the length of the first. It is easier to read, far less boring and contains all the same information.

Sounding dated or wordy

When we are learning to use language – at school, college, and university – we are encouraged to develop our vocabulary and grammar. Quite right too. If we didn't, we'd all be ignoramuses (or should that be ignorami?). As a result, we are often left with the impression that the longer a word and the more complex the sentence, the better.

If we are to be writers, and more importantly writers who are read, what we must learn is a sense of self-discipline. Education is there to develop us. I'm quite proud that I know the meanings of words like "meretricious" and "chthonic", but until just now I've never found a place to use them.

There's nothing wrong with good grammar (or long words). It helps to know the rules in order to break them. However, if you write your life story in the same style as you would have used for a school history essay, then it will make dull reading. And your first duty to your reader is to entertain. "Make 'em laugh, make 'em cry", as the saying goes. Of course you want to inform the reader about your life, but don't push that information to the front so that what you've written is a laundry list.

Language also has a nasty habit of dating very quickly. Victorian novelists had page upon page in which they could churn out complex sentences. The leisured classes who read their books had fewer distractions than the modern reader. Even books written only fifty years ago often seem very old-fashioned.

It's important to make your words resonate down the generations. If your life story already sounds as though it was written a hundred years ago, how dated will it sound in another fifty years?

To avoid this, try making your writing sound as though you are talking to the reader, then you will find that you end up with a readable style. It may not be the style that would have your English teacher whooping it up in the classroom, but you're not writing for her any more.

Embroidering on the Truth

I'm not sure whether this is a pitfall or something that should be advocated. I guess if you are trying to write an honest account of your life for your family, you need what you write to be as near the truth as you can make it.

I say "as near the truth as you can make it", because there is no doubt that truth is an individual matter. Ask three "neutral" eyes witnesses to give accounts of the same incident and you will end up with three different versions. You can, at best, give only your version of the truth.

On the other hand, if you are writing a work that is simply based on matters autobiographical, rather than aiming for accuracy, then you can allow yourself a far greater degree of flexibility as regards "the truth". Again, you need to tread very carefully. If your aunt, who is really the world's most generous soul, is portrayed as a stingy miser who allowed her daughter to sleep outside in a snowdrift, then you are straying into very dangerous territory indeed. You are now entering the world of libel.

Libel

Libel is a complicated subject, one that is well beyond the bounds of this book, but which is something that needs to be borne in mind nonetheless.

Essentially, you commit a libel if you make a defamatory statement about an identifiable living person, or a company that is still trading. "Identifiable" seems to be the key word, so even by disguising "Sowerby Brothers Meat Products" as "Southern Sisters Pork Pies", you may not be avoiding potential libel. Similarly, if you defame the character of your headteacher without once mentioning her name, but we can infer who that person is, you could also be committing a libel.

There are several defences to an accusation of libel.

First, you can plead "justification". In other words, that everything you wrote about that person was true. You probably need potential witnesses to back you up. Just because it has been widely reported by the press that Euphonius P. Buckwheat is a sexual pervert is no defence either. If in fact there is no evidence that poor old Mr. Buckwheat is a pervert, then you have committed a libel just as much as the source from which you repeated it.

Second, you can argue that what you have said is "fair comment". You are allowed to have opinions about people. However, you will also have to show that you acted without malice.

Your third line of defence is that of "privilege". This defence is normally used by newspapers and magazines when they publish something about, for instance, a member of parliament that they deem to be in the public interest.

The fourth and last line of defence probably won't apply to you. It is called "innocent dissemination" and is mainly applicable to broadcasting or internet companies who may have disseminated a libel, but without having anything to do with its creation.

There are sharks in the waters of libel. A libel case is often long, extremely expensive and even the winners don't seem to win. The only person to come out smiling in a libel case is a lawyer.

You can't libel the dead. However, if an inference can be made by descendants that what is said for the dead could also be applied to them, then you may have committed a libel. If you write "It's hardly surprising that Edmond Snodgrass was a snob. His father had been a snob and his father before him. So too were all the other Snodgrass relatives." Then, despite the fact that Edmond, Edmond's father and Edmond's grandfather are all dead, as are the relatives to whom you refer, I as Edmond Snodgrass's nephew, might take exception as I am a Snodgrass relative and you have clearly stated that I am a snob and I feel I am not. Unfortunately, "Oh, I didn't mean you" is probably no defence.

The Society of Authors (address in the appendix) publishes a handy little guide to libel. It currently costs £2.00 for non-members, but is available to members free of charge.

Of course, the best way to avoid a suit for libel, is not to libel anyone in the first place.

Copyright

We will deal with the matter of your own copyright in the next chapter. Here, we only need concern ourselves with other people's copyright.

If you print anything that you have not written yourself, you may be in breach of copyright.

Deliberately copying someone else's work verbatim is known as plagiarism and is frowned on in the extreme. If you publish anything that looks as though you have simply transferred paragraphs into your own manuscript and are passing it off as your own work, you could be heading for serious trouble. You can be sued for plagiarism, have your work forcibly withdrawn from sale – possibly pulped – and you could be in for some heavy financial losses.

Quoting from other works is, however, acceptable, providing you do so within strict limits. Limit yourself to 300-400 words from a single full-length book and a line or two of poetry and you shouldn't go too far wrong. If you want to use any more than this, then you must obtain the copyright owner's permission for which you will probably also be expected to pay a fee. This normally doesn't apply if an author has been dead for more than seventy years as their work should no longer be in copyright.

Remember a couple of other useful things:

You might want to reproduce photographs in your memoir. The person who took the photograph is normally the copyright holder, although this can vary. For instance, if the photograph was taken by an employee as part of his/her work for a company, then copyright probably rests with the company.

Copyright for letters remains with the person who wrote the letter, not the recipient. So, if you want to include a letter that was written to you, you need the copyright owner's permission.

As a rule of thumb, if in doubt, either seek permission or ask yourself if you really need this particular piece. You might be surprised at how much easier it is to go without something than it is to track down the copyright owner and then ask permission.

Chapter 7 - Preparing Your Manuscript
....

"I was working on the proof of one of my poems all morning, and took out a comma. In the afternoon, I put it back again." Oscar Wilde

Practical Issues for the Writer

If you have hand-written your work, it may be fine to keep as a memento, but if you want to do anything more with it, then you will definitely need a typed version. If you have the typing skills, or some knowledge of computers, you can do this yourself.

Typing up your own work can be a very useful process. Some writers I know, hand-write their early drafts and then type these up (usually onto a computer) themselves. Somehow, they feel comfortable writing with pen and paper– it's what they were brought up on. Then, when they transfer their hand-written story to the computer, they can make changes as they do so. This means that the first draft soon becomes a second draft. What appears on their computer screens has already had some revising, editing and polishing.

If you are thinking about publishing your life story – in any form – then access to technology is vital. Occasionally, you will hear of editors accepting a handwritten piece from someone, but in the main, no magazine or publishing company is going to take a second look at anything that isn't typed. The very minimum you can get away with is a typewriter. Frankly, you're much better off with a computer.

Nowadays, I write directly onto a computer most of the time. If I don't have access to a computer, I may hand-write, but I suffer quickly from writer's cramp when I do. The second reason I write directly onto the computer is that I am hopeless at copy typing. I never learned to type properly and, although over the years I've developed a nifty seven-finger typing style that is reasonably effective, I have to watch the keyboard at all times, otherwise the letters on it miraculously swap places.

There are huge advantages in having your work on a computer. If you type your manuscript on a type-writer and then decide to add a couple of paragraphs, it probably means re-typing the whole manuscript. With a computer, if I want to do this, I can easily insert text. If I want to move some information from page eight to page eighty, I can do so with a handful of keyboard strokes or a flash of the mouse.

If you can't type and have never used a computer, there are dozens of courses available at local adult education centres and further education colleges. Computers are also tumbling in price all the time, so you can pick up a bargain almost everywhere you look.

There are also computer programmes available that allow you to dictate your work directly into a computer using a microphone. These programmes are called "dictation software" and can be bought at most computer shops. If you use this technique, then you may find it easiest to handwrite your stories first, then read them into the computer, otherwise you may find that your life story largely consists of "ums" and "ers".

However, if you don't want to do your own typing and have an aversion to machines, there are plenty of people who will be able to do it for you. A wanted advert in your local paper, or in a shop window, should find you someone who can do the job for you. I know a young woman with small children who does occasional typing from home on her computer. It's ideal for her, as she can fit the work in round family commitments and great for her customers, who are able to get good quality work at a reasonable price.

If you decide to use a typing service, make sure that you ask for your work to be returned to you as both "hard copy" and disk. For those unused to these terms, what this means is that you want a copy of what you've written printed out on paper, and also saved electronically onto a computer disk. If the paper copy goes missing or is damaged, then you can always have another copy printed from the disk.

Always make sure you have copies of what you've written. If you do your work on the computer, always make a back-up onto disk. I speak from bitter experience. Writing my first book, I lost an entire chapter. I still don't think that my "new" version was as good as the first.

If you're not writing onto a computer, you can photocopy handwritten pages at your local library or often at a corner shop. It may increase the cost of your project, but if your master copy goes missing, then you've got a spare.

So, let's assume that you now have your work on a computer, what are you going to do with it?

Selling Excerpts from Your Life Story as Articles

As the average age of the population increases, so too does the boom in magazines aimed at the older market. This has meant a growth in the market for nostalgia articles.

Now, don't think that this means that nostalgia articles are easy to sell. As with all sectors of the market, editors are flooded with work. Some of it is highly useable; a great deal is terrible dross.

A while back, I was talking to the editor of a well-known regional magazine. He told me that he was inundated with twee pieces telling all about the author's schooldays in the area It wasn't that he would never publish a piece on someone's schooldays, it's just that the piece would either have to be by someone well-known or would have to be so wonderful that he couldn't resist it.

Look round the shelves of your local magazine shop. Titles such as "Evergreen", "This England", "The Oldie", and "The People's Friend" are all aimed at the older age group. I am sure you will discover a dozen more besides; there's a big market out there.

You may also often read an article in a magazine and think "So what? I could write that." I used to do this all the time and it was, in fact, my excuse for not writing anything. So, if you ever see an article and think "I could have written that", then ask yourself "why didn't I?" and knuckle down to write some equivalent piece.

Before sending anything to a magazine, you need to study at least three editions of the magazine. This is to get the "flavour" of it. Some magazines have a cosy, chatty style; others are deliberately abrasive and interested in abseiling grannies rather than knitting patterns. Look at the adverts, read the letters page , immerse yourself in the "feel" of the magazine. Do you have a piece that would fit?

Also, check out the details of the magazine in one of the annual writer's guides (See Handbooks in Appendix A). See if they take freelance contributions. Some don't; others may be entirely freelance-written. Don't forget that many professional associations have their own in-house magazines that may offer you a home for an article.

You will need to tailor any article you write for its potential home. If a magazine has a slot for nostalgia articles of 800 words, it's pointless sending them one of 2,000. If a magazine never prints poems, there is no point in writing "I know you never normally print poems, but I'm sure that this one about the death of my cat Tiddles will touch a nerve with many of your readers."

Once you have found a likely target for your work and adjusted your piece to suit that magazine, you need to present your work professionally to the editor.

Print out your finished article in double-space, with a good wide margin of around 3.5 cms (1 ½ inches) all the way round. Make sure you number the pages. If you are typing, rather than using a computer, keep Tippex to a minimum.

Type a covering sheet that states simply your name and address, the title of the article and include the words "FBSR Offered". FBSR stands for "First British Serial Rights" and essentially means that you are offering the magazine the first rights to publish this article in a periodical. Somewhere at the foot of the page, it is reasonable to include your name and the copyright symbol. However, don't splatter the copyright symbol all over the place. It is the sign of the over-anxious amateur, terrified lest the wicked editor is going to rip off his wonderful idea. Frankly, my experience has shown that the more anxious someone has been about their idea being stolen, the poorer that idea is. Editors have probably had the same experience. They're inundated with material and are looking for reasons NOT to publish your work.

Write a straightforward covering letter. Don't try to be clever, coy or too jokey. Use the editor's name and, if the editor is a woman, find out if she likes being addressed as Miss, Mrs. or Ms. Sign off with "Yours Sincerely". Don't use a pen-name unless you are writing about something that is hugely personal and you need to keep your identity a secret. Pen names are for amateurs and the kinds of prolific novelists who write in different genres and so have different readerships.

Don't forget to include a stamped self-addressed envelope for the editor's reply. This is regarded as a common courtesy. Some magazines will get 100 or more unsolicited submissions a week. If magazines bore the cost of replying to them all, then they would soon be out of business.

If you haven't had a reply from the magazine within 6-8 weeks, it is reasonable to follow up with a query letter. It's probably best to avoid phoning editors. They don't like interruptions and may feel as though you are hassling them. If you get no reply, then re-work the piece and send it to the next magazine on your hit list.

Writing for magazines can be very rewarding. Whilst you are unlikely to make a personal fortune from it, some magazines do pay quite handsomely for well-written pieces that their readers will enjoy. There is no reason why you couldn't use extracts from your life story as a springboard for developing a part-time career writing about all sorts of different issues for magazines.

Publishing Your Life Story

You may, however, feel that rather than trying to sell extracts – or indeed as well as selling extracts – from your work, you would like to see your finished work in some kind of permanent form.

This could range from simple home publishing, to attempting to sell your book to a publisher. Let's look at some of these options.

Home Publishing

For most of you reading this book, home publishing will be what you are aiming to do. You will be recording parts of your life for your children and grandchildren, so that they know what your experiences were.

You can make your home-published book as inexpensive or as dear as you want. The cheapest way to produce a "book" is to print on A4 pages, then use a hole punch and a ribbon to tie the whole together.

A step up from this is to use some kind of plastic binding. Most "copy shops" and a large number of libraries have the facilities to put some kind of plastic binder on your finished work. In fact, binding machines are now so cheap, that you could probably share the cost of one round a writers' group (if you belong to one), or pick one up second-hand and re-sell it when you've finished.

If you're looking for something a little grander, there are specialist binders in almost every university town who put together dissertations and doctoral theses. If you're only producing a handful of presentation copies, this might be worth the added expense. In fact, what could be a greater personalised present than giving your family a handsomely bound copy of your life story?

Submitting your work to an agent or publisher

Some of you may be more ambitious. You might think that your story deserves a wider audience.

It may well do, but if you're going down the route of trying to find an agent or a publisher, you have to be prepared to be disappointed. If selling articles is hard, then selling a full-scale book is even harder.

The story of your life may make fascinating reading for your family, but that does not mean that it will make fascinating reading for the wider public.

Publishing is a commercial business. Publishers need to make a profit in order to survive.

Agents and publishers are inundated with material. For every "Angela's Ashes" they see, they have to sift through a thousand or more stories that range from the inept and the banal to the near misses.

Yes, we all know the tales of the masterpiece that was rejected by seventy-five publishers. Unfortunately, whilst there may be a rare exception, books that are rejected repeatedly with nothing more than a standard rejection letter are normally rejected for good reasons.

Of course, if you've followed the advice in this book, you stand a better chance than most. So, if you can withstand the battering that trying to sell your work to publishers can inflict on your ego, then here's what you have to do.

First of all, there's a bit of a Catch 22 in publishing. It's difficult to get a book published without an agent and difficult to get an agent without a book deal in place. If this is the only book you intend writing, then you probably don't need an agent. To begin with, stick to finding a publisher. You can always interest an agent at a later stage if you are suddenly offered a world-beating deal.

Make a list of publishers who might be interested in your work. Get down to your library and local bookshop and identify which publishers produce books like yours. You can find out more about which publishers to approach using one of the annual guides for writers, "The Writer's Handbook" or "The Writers' and Artists' Yearbook". Some will only be interested in approaches from agents. Forget them for the time being and concentrate on those who will accept unsolicited manuscripts.

Most of those publishers who can be approached without an agent ask for a sample of your writing and a synopsis. Publishers (or agents for that matter) do not want to see an entire manuscript at first. They want to know that you can write and that you have a good story to tell. They can probably do that from one page of your writing. In fact, PFD, the largest agency in the country, asks children's authors to submit just one paragraph from their book, along with a synopsis. That's how tough it can be.

As a rule of thumb, send two or three chapters at most, along with a short covering letter and a brief synopsis of your book. Your synopsis should tell the reader about the main characters and events in the book. It should also be interesting. Writing a synopsis is hard work. It is your calling card. Spend time working it up into an interesting little read in its own right. Would the synopsis tempt you to read the book?

You then need to write a covering letter. This should be kept simple, stating the title of the book and any relevant information. Don't try to be clever, funny or over-elaborate. What you are sending is a business proposal. It needs to be crisp and to the point.

I always enclose a stamped addressed envelope. I state in my covering letter that I don't want the manuscript back. That way, I can save on postage and can buy smaller, cheaper envelopes for the return letter. There's also little point in getting back a manuscript that is dog-eared and covered in coffee stains.

Don't fold your manuscript. If it is too large to paper-clip, simply slip an elastic band around it. Whatever else you do, do not put pretty pink ribbons on it and avoid those plastic wallets – people in publishing don't like them as they tend to slide off desks and filing cabinets.

Then, send your chapters and synopsis, together with a covering letter to the first half-dozen publishers on your list.

Publishers don't particularly like this, but I think it's something they have to learn to live with. Sometimes a publisher will sit on a manuscript for as long as six months. Frankly, you can't wait that long for an outcome. When I tell my students this, they always worry about what might happen if two publishers are interested in the same book. I always tell them that this sounds like an ideal world. If you're selling your house and two people are interested in it, then that's bound to push up the price. Having two publishers interested looks to me like a problem that is worth trying to handle.

Make sure you keep a good record of where you have sent your work. As each rejection comes in (and they will), then send your pack to the next publisher on your list.

Be prepared to suffer rejection; all writers are rejected at some point or other. You have to be prepared for it. Rejection is hard to take. I had a rejection letter the morning I was writing this section of the book. I guess it must have been at least my 200th and it still hurt. You feel as though a little part of you is being rejected.

One of the difficulties with rejection is that it is rare for either magazine editors or publishers to give a reason for it. Quite simply, it's not their job. Nor is it their job to explain to us what we could do to a piece to make it of publishable standard. If they did that, then they wouldn't have time to do any publishing or editing.

Most letters are standard rejection letters. They are normally polite, but restrained and use words like "not suitable" and explain how many zillions of submissions they have each day. Occasionally, an editor or publisher will come back with something a little more personal. "I really liked the tone of this, but we did a similar piece in issue 66" is an indication that you have a potentially saleable item on your hands. See these kinds of rejections in as positive a light as you can. They are genuine near-misses. Next time, you might be luckier.

Self-publishing

If you find that you are rejected by every publisher in the book, then you might think of publishing the book yourself. By this, I mean that you might want to produce what you have written as something more than a bound manuscript. You want your book to look just like the ones that appear on the shelves in the shops.

Self-publishing has a long and illustrious history. Beatrix Potter published the first edition of "Peter Rabbit" using her own money. Virginia Wolf published several of her works herself. However, these were wealthy, upper middle-class ladies, who could afford to self-publish and lose a few bob without having to worry about the mortgage.

Self-publishing a book is an expensive business. Before you leap into it, just take time to think about it. If you can afford to lose all the money that such a venture will cost you, then go ahead and do it. You'll find it is a lot of fun. But be prepared to have a garage full of boxes of books when your self-published memoir simply doesn't sell.

If you are considering self-publishing, it is well-worth buying one or more of the several excellent books there are on the subject. You must not go into such a venture blithely, but aware of how time and money consuming it can be.

However, if you're thinking of producing a shorter volume, say one of 10,000 words, one that has strong local connections, then producing a less-ambitious volume, say of 32 to 64 pages in A5 format is a possibility. Approach local printers for a price. Whatever they tell you it will cost per unit, you then need to put a cover price of around four times that amount to ensure that you cover all your costs and allow for discounts to shops, etc. You will find that the unit cost of each book will be cheaper the more you have printed. Be realistic. If you think you can sell 200 copies, have 200 copies printed. You can always have extras made. It may make the unit cost more expensive, but it is preferable to having 1,000 booklets sitting rotting in the garden shed.

Vanity Publishing

If you decide to self-publish a book, you are in charge of its production. There are companies who will take over the process for you and provide you with however many copies you want. These companies are entirely respectable printing businesses who take on the extra duties of obtaining an ISBN number, typesetting, design and so on.

However, there are some sharks in these waters. They are often referred to as "vanity publishers", because, quite simply, they play on our vanity. They tell us that our manuscript is "remarkable", "refreshing", "the best thing I have read in years". They dangle likely sales figures that are way in excess of anything you're honestly, likely to achieve. Then they sting you for a "contribution to printing costs".

The autobiographer is an easy prey for a vanity publisher. We all think our story should be read by the widest possible audience. When it is turned down by the umpteenth publisher, you turn to those you'll have to pay yourself to publish. You have put so much of yourself – your time, let's face it, your life – into this book, that it is going to see the light of day no matter what.

The excellent Jonathon Clifford has been running a campaign for many years to put an end to the worst excesses of vanity publishing.

On his website, he quotes the British Standards Authority, who describe vanity publishers as "any company which charges a client to publish a book; or offers to include short stories, poems or other literary or artistic material in an anthology and then invites those included to buy a copy of that anthology." The trouble with vanity presses is that they can easily suck you in. I know of one elderly gentleman, a veteran of the beaches of Dunkirk, who lost a thousand pounds when a "subsidy publisher" (another name by which they lurk) went bust.

There are also horror stories of people parting with even more money than this to find that, yes, they do have 2,000 copies of their book, but the essential clause that said the pages of their book would be bound together was missing from the contract. What they've really got is 350,000 sheets of paper.

Mainstream publishers are generally realistic when it comes to selling your book. OK, occasionally they shell out ludicrous sums for works by well-known TV stars and footballers, but in the main they can tell how many copies a book will sell. Vanity publishers will talk you up - there's no limit to the number of copies of your book they will sell. Be very careful. There's a thin line between vanity publishers and people who will genuinely help you self-publish your book. If you're thinking of self-publishing and you're looking for a company to do it for you, then ask them to put you in touch with other customers.

Final Word

Selling anything autobiographical to magazines, agents or publishers is hard work. There are thousands of people just like yourself out there, who have important stories to tell. Don't be dismayed if you find that no-one wants to publish your work for commercial gain. Simply produce a smart homemade folder of your work, written to the highest possible standards you can achieve, and your family will be left with an amazing record of your life.

Chapter 8 – Some Examples

....
.

The past is a foreign country; they do things differently there. L.P. Hartley "The Go-between"

This chapter contains a selection of examples of writing taken from amongst my students.

I've provided a little commentary after each excerpt, explaining what I like about each piece. You might disagree with my thoughts – you're entitled to. However, where you like the way in which someone has written a section – a description, a character sketch, whatever - don't be frightened to imitate what you read.

Any analysis of a piece of writing can quickly make it seem like we're discussing how a car engine works. Writing isn't that mechanical. I don't suppose when my students wrote these extracts they said to themselves things like "I must introduce a person here in order to add interest". It's almost instinctive. But, when you see some of the techniques in operation and then practise them yourself, you will soon absorb them and then do them without thinking.

The pieces are presented here in no particular order. I hope you enjoy reading them and that my comments make reasonable sense.

An Ashington Childhood – Evelyn Rutherford

Smoke from a nearby chimney drifts across the garden. A rare occurrence in these days of smokeless zones and clean fuels. I sniff the sooty cloud and I am a child again in the Northeast town of Ashington, in the centre of the Northumbrian coalfields. Woodhorn, Felham Down, Lynemouth, Pegwood, Longhirst, North Seaton, Ellington and more. All names of mines in a radius of about seven miles, with Ashington in the centre. All gone, but now imprinted on my mind forever.

"Ashington is the biggest mining village in the world,"
Miss Green, a teacher at junior school, told us one day. With a
population of 27,000 in the 1950s, it could hardly be still
classed as a village, but none of us would argue with Miss
Green, an ugly woman who wore a wig and a hair-net on top to
stop it from blowing off in the wind.

With so many mines in the vicinity, pit shafts, wheels,
large buildings and enormous chimneys dominated the skyline
around Ashington. Machinery clanked day and night and the
massive wheels turned continuously as they hauled up their
cargoes from deep beneath the earth. Steam trains hissed and
hooted as they were shunted onto sidetracks waiting for their
trucks to be filled.

One of the first things to strike me about this extract is
the way in which Evelyn uses the senses to evoke a sense of
place. She even uses her sense of smell to start the piece. She
smells smoke and is transported to childhood Ashington. It's a
famous literary trick. Marcel Proust does it in "Remembrance of
Things Past", when he dunks his Madeleine cake in his coffee
and is immediately transported to childhood. It's a great example
of how to use a flashback very early on in a piece to get your
story moving.

This particular flashback not only allows us to re-enter
the world of the colliery village, but also hints at the difference
between the world back then and the way it is as Evelyn is
writing.

Writing lists is always a tricky business. But lists in a piece
of autobiography can work if they're used sparingly. Here,
Evelyn's list of the names of mines evokes the kind of list
memorised in childhood. It's almost like reciting a times table, or
even a mantra.

Introducing people – characters – into your writing is
essential. Evelyn could simply have written "Ashington was the
biggest mining village in the world back then". She hasn't, she's
chosen to put the words into the mouth of her junior school

teacher, and to give as an amusing thumb-nail sketch of the woman at the same time.

I like this short description. It's very easy to get carried away every time you introduce a new character and give the reader far more detail than they can cope with. The information that Miss Green is ugly and keeps her wig on with a hair-net is short, sharp, to the point and has a humorous slant to it.

Home Cooking – Jim Billsborough

Sal was manageress of the art college canteen. Eggs and chips, Cornish pasty with baked beans and Scotch eggs all made regular guest appearances on the menu. But as a special treat, Sal sometimes did a bit of home cooking. Especially popular were her rock buns. Students bought them by the dozen, painted them in colourful, jazzy designs and sold them as novelty paperweights, though the larger ones were only really suitable as doorstops.

It's hardly fair to sneer at Sal's culinary skills for she could display a much lighter touch. For example, in the car-owning community, men could be seen out in force on a Sunday morning, washing the sleek lines of their nearest and dearest with a slice of her chocolate sponge cake, oozing creamy, soapy water.

However, her pastries and pies weren't quite so popular as they appealed only to students with an aptitude for archaeology. One such student, using the most primitive of tools, claimed he had to excavate over two inches of pastry before he came across what he took to be a small piece of chicken. He sent it to the laboratory for analysis. They reported it to be pterodactyl Quite tasty in itself, but definitely not chicken. The Environmental Health Officer had no option but to condemn Sal's pie as unfit for human consumption: carbon-dating had confirmed it was well past its sell-by date.

Humour is a very personal thing. What has one person roaring with laughter can leave another person cold. Jim's piece certainly didn't leave me cold; I think it's uproariously funny.

I think that Jim has broken the rules here, and got away with it. It would have been so easy to say "Sal's cooking was awful" and leave it at that, but what he does is take us on a ridiculous, surreal journey through Sal's menu.

Of course, none of this is "true" in the sense that this is exactly what happened in Sal's canteen. However, it is true in the sense that what Sal made was largely inedible and often stale. It's through this extreme over-exaggeration that Jim gets the effect he wants. It's quite P.G. Wodehouse-meets- Spike Milligan.

One of the dangers of writing comedy is that you can end up being cruel. I suspect that if Jim had written more conventionally about how bad Sal's cooking was, it would have been a far crueller depiction than it is by using over-exaggeration.

Comedy is extremely difficult to write – which is why the writers of successful sitcoms and funny films often end up rolling in filthy lucre. By all means try writing in a comic voice, but don't be upset if you don't manage it. It really is a tough skill. Conversely, if you find yourself writing in a comic tone and think that somehow you should be writing in a serious voice, then think again. The fact that comic writing comes easily to you is a skill to be treasured, not discarded. The clown doesn't have to play Hamlet.

George by Pat Graham

George died last year.

He died of alcohol abuse. That's what they put on his death certificate.

I felt I died with him.

I can't remember when I first became aware of having a brother. He was always there. His name was George and he was my Big Brother. I loved him with a passion and fierceness; he was and always will be my hero.

I envied him his beautiful blond hair, which was almost white, his blue eyes like my mother's and grandfather's – blue like the sky on an endless summer's day, his dimples, his friendly manner and easygoing ways, but most of all his kindness and capacity to love.

Pat Graham opens this pen portrait of her brother with the simplest of statements. "George died last year".

It is a straightforward, clear message that gets its information over to us immediately. It also makes us begin to ask questions. Who is George? What relation is he to Pat? Is he important in her life? How did he die? Was he young? Was he old? Could George even have been a "she" rather than a "he"?

The short sentences, the simple but honest sentiments - we are with Pat all the way and we want to know more about George. What was he like? How come he ended up an alcoholic?

It's interesting to note the way in which the cold, short, declarative sentences of the first few lines are in direct contrast to the free-flowing emotional writing of the last paragraph. In fact, this short extract pivots round the line "I felt I died with him", a feeling that is often felt by people when a loved one dies.

Pat's description of George is seen through her eyes, making both George and Pat, as the writer, come alive to the reader. There is the mixture of childish envy of his hair and eyes, the reference to him as "Big Bruther" and more mature envy of his easy-going nature.

Bicycle Accident by Rita Bell

It was in Coldharbour Lane that I had my first accident with the bike, when I crashed into a stationary car. The driver had stopped abruptly without warning. He was indifferent to anything other than the condition of his car. He got out, examined his car, got in, drove off. He left me shivering and stunned lying in the middle of a very busy road with lorries and cars skidding and swerving to avoid me. Crying with shock

,I felt conspicious in my blue uniform. Not a soul seemed prepared to come and help me.

As I lay there, I could hear women's voices. "Oh look, Mabel, there's someone over there, she's had an accident. Do you think we ought to ...?"

"Get an ambulance? No, it's OK, Dot, she's a nurse. We can't help her. She'll know all that first aid stuff."

"Yeah. She'll sort herself out Come on, don't hang about. I thought you wanted to get down the market."

"In the block of flats opposite, Mr. Bowman was looking out of the window, waiting for me to call and give him his injection. On seeing the accident, he made his way down the stairs to help. Although in his early seventies, his recent marriage to a woman half his age and a regular dosage of ginseng had given him the agility of a far younger man. He scurried down the stairs to the rescue, helped me out of the road and up the stone steps to his spotless little flat. He could see I was shocked and shaken and suggested a cup of tea.

"Why not take off your shoes, Nurse, and have a rest on my bed?"

By now he was gasping for breath, having tackled several flights of stairs. I had a head that felt like it was in the grip of a Sumo wrestler. The offer was too tempting to decline.

"Just you relax on the bed, love. I'll get you a nice cuppa. My wife will be back in a minute."

There was something about the last remark that attempted to penetrate my inert mind. Weariness silenced it. A key turned slowly in the lock. Despite my dazed state, in an instant I could visualise the scenario:

Young wife walks in – nurse lying on bed – husband breathless.

It had all the ingredients of a compromising situation. Pulse racing, I leapt off the bed, forced my stockinged feet into laced up shoes, hastily adjusted my uniform and quickly called *out "It's all right, Mr. Bowman, I feel a lot better now. I'll come in the kitchen for that cup of tea."*

I just managed to slither into the kitchen as his wife was hanging up her coat in the hallway.

One of the real strengths of Rita's writing – and I think this is shown in this piece – is how easy she makes it for us to read her work. Her writing has a lightness of touch to it that is worth striving for in your own. She also gets that mixture of dialogue, description, characterisation and narration exactly right; as she does the mixture of bathos and humour.

It would be very easy to turn the accident into a long moan about how painful and upsetting the experience was. Rita avoids this. Yes, we feel a certain sympathy for her and, had she wanted to, she could have made the indifference of the driver and bystanders into a huge commentary about the way in which not enough people are prepared to look out for others. Instead, she doesn't. She keeps herself as the object of the humour. Yes, it is wrong that they don't help, but we're quickly moving on from that to the incident in Mr. Bowman's flat.

This incident actually happened. However, the way Rita originally wrote it, she (as a young nurse) just lay on the bed and wondered what would happen if the new young wife had come home to find her there. After some discussion, we decided that it was fine to play around with the "truth" a little to make the story have more impact, so Rita had the wife arriving home.

I like the way that Rita chooses to write "Young wife walks in – nurse lying on bed – husband breathless", writing it as though she were telling this as an anecdote round a pub table. It makes the end result far snappier, and because we are given the impression that she is talking to us, we are drawn into her world.

Our Shetland Home by Norma Brannan

There was no sign of the road indicating Olna; just a lane to the right leading to the water. Two houses sat snugly on the hillside and I parked beside the one named "Olna Cottage".

The half-acre of land around the building had obviously not seen a spade for years. It was a terraced tangle of weeds and wildflowers and I counted three wild rosebushes in full bloom emerging from the wilderness by the back door.

At the front of the house, the ground fell away into a meadow leading to the shores of Olna Firth. Apart from a half-finished pier and a boat moving towards a solitary fishing farm, there was nothing to detract from the view and the only sounds the mournful cries of seabirds. Across the Firth, lay the uninhabited peninsula of Grobsness, its contours reflected in the unusually flat, calm waters; a scene that had probably remained unchanged for centuries.

I felt a sense of homecoming never experienced before. Having dreamt for years of an isolated house close to the water, with a boat moored at the end of the garden, here it was. Such dreams rarely materialise. I knew I had to have this house and, suddenly remembering that I had an appointment to view it, went to the door.

It is very easy to describe places badly. This is not the case with Norma's restrained description of Shetland. Here, I think Norma has managed to avoid the most obvious trap and that is to give a static description, so that what she is describing is a postcard, rather than a moving image.

She has achieved this by threading herself into the description. She quickly introduces herself to the description and then becomes the camera through which we see this little house. She gives her point-of-view, both in the cinematic sense, and in the sense that we know how she feels about this place. She loves this place, and that comes through from the writing. In fact she loves it so much, that she even forgets that she has come to view the house.

Note also, that although this is an entirely descriptive piece, Norma has not laid on the adjective-adverb trowel too thickly. The two houses "sat snugly"

The garden "had not seen a spade in years". The seabirds give off "mournful cries" (use of sound to appeal to more than one sense). So, she builds up a picture using little brush-strokes and allows us to colour in a lot of the rest using our own imaginations.

This is a short piece, but already Norma has built up a picture of it. We also get the feeling that we are going to learn more about the house and Norma's relationship with it. We want to know what life is going to be like somewhere this isolated, when the waters of the Olna Firth are not flat and calm. Some of this is already flagged up for us. We can see that there is going to be a tussle taming the wilderness garden and the way that garden falls away makes us wonder if something untoward might happen here.

It's a neat bit of introductory description.

Visiting Mother by Maureen Toyn

Here am I, now a grandmother, going to visit a great-grandmother, who was once my lovely, lively Mother.

I drive up to the home, which is pleasantly situated overlooking the sea. Taking my offerings of fruit and books, I make my way into the residents' lounge.

There she sits. She's in full flow, to a retired headmistress, about the decline in the town since her youth. I stand in front of her waiting for recognition.

"Here you are, then. Did you have a good journey?" She's sure that each trip will be the last for us as she is appalled at how much traffic there is on the road.

"Yes thank you, I ..."

"Alan's got a new car. It's a BMX."

"A BMX is a bicycle."

"This is a car."

114

I gaze around the room and it doesn't seem such a bad place to be, but mother can't wait to be home again from this respite care.

"Mrs. Jones came to visit me the other day. Her daughter's having trouble getting pregnant. They've paid a lot of money for her to have MFI treatment."

"I think you mean IVF, don't you."

"That can't be right, it's a TV station."

"You're thinking of ITV."

"Oh, I get all mixed up when everything is initials these days. We'll forget how to speak properly soon. See that lady over there? She's got necromancy, poor thing. Keeps dropping off to sleep at a moment's notice."

I find I haven't the vocabulary to explain the difference between "necromancy" and "narcolepsy", so I let that one go.

Maureen wanted to capture the way in which her mother is always using malapropisms. However, she had a tightrope to walk with the humour of the piece. If she didn't get the tone quite right, it would sound as though she was mocking her elderly mother for being forgetful.

I think she's got the balance between finding her mother's misuse of language – especially acronyms – and the obvious care that she feels towards her mother about right. The fact that she brings fruit and books for her mother and that her mother is worried about the possibility of her daughter being in a car crash mean that the relationship is more than just having a giggle at a forgetful old lady. Of course, the old lady is worrying about the car far more than she needs to, but it still shows she cares.

I also like the simplicity of the description. We get a picture of the respite care home from just one or two tiny snippets of information. It is "pleasantly situated overlooking the sea" and "it doesn't seem such a bad place to be". We don't really need any more information than that, because we now the kind of place Maureen's talking about. We can fill in those extra details for ourselves. Besides, it's the relationship with her mother that the piece is exploring, not the nursing home.

What a great last line in which Maureen realises that, whilst she knows the difference between "necromancy" and "narcolepsy", she can't explain it. The joke is now on the writer.

A Bigger Garden by Heather Graves

"For Christ's sake, Geoff, all I wanted was a bigger garden!"

I glared belligerently at my husband of fourteen years, trying not to think where my left hand was. The old ewe's rasping breath warmed the icy air, her flesh defrosting my fingers. A feeble sun failed to dent the brittle, white crust on the fields. My fields.

"I can't believe I'm doing this,"I muttered through clenched teeth. Tidy, organised Carol, with her neat edges and orderly life. Lover of boundaries, fences around things. Thrust blindfold into this chaotic world of crumbling walls, sprawling unkempt acres and livestock, for God's sake, all demanding attention.

"I think I've got a leg, Geoff!"

"Good lass, now find the other one and pull like hell!"

No white fluffiness here; a steaming bloodied streak of new life slithered onto the frozen ground before me.

"Just a bigger bloody garden," I whispered to nobody in particular. The ewe stared at me, unmoved. Our new lives spluttered into being together.

When I was at school, I was taught that you should never start a story with dialogue. I've got no idea why I was taught such rubbish, but there you go. Dialogue is a great way to start a piece. Here, Heather sets up the situation in one short exclamatory sentence. "For Christ's sake, Geoff, all I wanted was a bigger garden." You can hear the exasperation in the sentence and are drawn in to wonder what the narrator has ended up with if all she wanted was a bigger garden.

Then we are cleverly drop-fed information. She's been married fourteen years where is that left hand? She's doing something with an old ewe, we're not exactly sure what it is, but we guess it's to do with lambing, so we read on and "I think I've got a leg, Geoff" – once again proving how a short, sharp piece of dialogue can work the trick. Yes, it's lambing We were right. "My fields." What have they done. She wanted a bigger garden and they've bought – what? A smallholding? A farm? Half of Herefordshire? Anyway, there are "sprawling, unkempt acres", so it must be bigger than your average suburban garden. A lot bigger.

And within all this, there are smidgens of description to help us locate where we are. "A feeble sun failed to dent the brittle, white crust on the fields." Much sharper writing than "It was cold, frosty and the fields belonged to me." Now we're getting more of a picture. Then, when the lamb is finally born, we're not told it's a lamb; it's a "bloodied streak of new life". This last, capturing the messiness and magic of new life wonderfully well. There's sensory description here we feel the cold and hear the "rasping breath" of the ewe as well as being given visual description.

We also learn something about our narrator. She's not above a bit of blaspheming and swearing. She's also normally a tidy, organised person. She's now coping with the chaos of life in the raw – the real countryside. We also seem to be fictionalised to some extent – the narrator is a woman called Carol and not the Heather who is the author of the piece.

We're also left with a little foreshadowing of what is to come. "Our new lives spluttered into being together." So, we know we're in for a story of how a green-fingered townie is going to cope with running some kind of a farm. We're probably going to get a flashback or some back story now.

Sugar Puffs and Marzines by Susan Stokes

I cannot eat a bowl of sugar puffs without feeling very, very sick.

Perhaps it was the cold that made me shiver, or just the excitement of being woken by my mother at 4 a.m. to a chorus of Tyneside foghorns blasting forth eerily in the distance. Attempting to control my chattering teeth, I slid from my cosy bed into the cold dawn of 1957.

Clothes were hastily pulled on, numb fingers fought with rubber buttons on liberty bodices. Prickly hand-knitted woollies were pulled over yawning mouths.

The great adventure had begun. Before me lay a ten-hour drive to Buckinghamshire to visit my grandparents.

Half-an-hour later and ready to go, I stood meekly before my parents, with dread in my heart, knowing what was to come.

"Go and get the Marzines, darling!"

Now Marzines were cunning little anti-travel-sickness pills that actually made you feel sick without the benefit of a car. Not only that, but they were packaged in a small tube with a swirly black-and-white top. This created a severe disorientation that could only be mimicked today by imbibing several large vodkas.

My mother, innovative as her generation was, and long before the era of the Little Chef, created her travelling breakfast. This consisted of a cardboard box filled with cereal bowls, milk, and a large packet of sugar puffs, all to be consumed in a lay-by two hours down the road.

Needless to say, two hours down the road with the smell of leather seats and the Marzines doing their worst, I would be roused by my mother and offered a large bowl of the offending cereal swimming in luke warm milk.

How such memories can colour lives.

It would be very easy to condense this little story into a line or two. By filling out what is a small episode into a larger story, it begins to reveal a great deal more about the character of both the narrator and her mother than "I still hate sugar puffs because I used to be forced to eat them on car journeys and they made me sick" would do. We learn that the mother is resourceful. The Marzines are well intentioned, but ultimately a mistake. There is a rigidity in the way she is to stick to her time-table.

The narrator, whilst admiring her mother's innovation, can't help feeling somewhat the victim of the whole process. "I stood meekly before my parents".

Here the narrator has mixed in the cleverness of adult hindsight, with some of the world of the child. The child's view is "The great adventure had begun". The adult's perspective "This created a severe disorientation that could only be mimicked today by imbibing several large vodkas".

Don't do it yourself by Cath Sweeney

Spending the weekend as builder's assistant, passing drills and screwdrivers, holding ladders and selecting appropriate bits to suit size 8, one and a half inch, plain slotted steel screws (it's easy after years of practice) made me muse on do-it-yourself incidents that have influenced my life. Some I remember clearly, others have become part of family folk legend.

When only a few months old I was left in the charge of my father for an afternoon. Being keen to get on with some repair job in the bedroom, and, at a loss for what to do with me, he opened the large bottom draw of the dresser, removed some of the contents and placed me carefully inside. All would have been well if my six year old brother had not closed the drawer. Even now, nearly fifty years on, he has never really accepted or come to terms with me.

Up to the age of seven we still had gas lighting at home. Not that electricity wasn't available, we were the odd ones out, everybody round about us had it. My father had a pal, a friend of long standing, who dabbled in electricity. If anybody was going to install electric he was going to do it, he said. 'Over my dead body', said my mother. She was remembering the day that she had gone out shopping and returned to find the kitchen in utter chaos. Being at a loose end my dad's pal had come round and suggested that while she was out they should demolish the wall between the kitchen and the scullery to create an airy, open kitchen; one that any wife would be proud to own.

'OK', said my dad, and they set about it there and then.

You can understand her reservations.

My dad was heavily involved in amateur dramatics. When asked what we'd bought our dad for Christmas or his birthday we'd reply, 'Make-up, of course'. Pan stick and Leichner no 8 being the preferred items.

My dad's pal did the electrics for the drama company and his master plan for our house was to have a control board by the front door, with switches for all the lights in the house, with labels, just as they had in the wings at the theatre.

"Over my dead body," said my mother, even more emphatically. My big brother was allowed to light the gas lights but I was not. On the very few occasions that I was allowed to try, despite being as careful as I could I would stab the mantle with the match and the ephemeral orb would disintegrate much to everybody's dismay. My Mother eventually arranged to have the electricity board install electric and presented it as a fait accompli. I was seven when we got electric, it arrived on a Monday, a television set arrived on the Wednesday and a hamster on the Friday. The three may not necessarily be connected.

This short extract shows just how inventive you can be even when taking something as mundane as DIY. From this piece, we don't just learn about her Dad's obsession with DIY, but a great deal about his attitude to life (and DIY) and her mother's attitude to him. Along the way, we also get snippets of colour – the brother closing the drawer with a tiny Cath inside. The ritual of the lighting of the gas mantles – so delicate that it was a job that couldn't be trusted to the youngest of the family.

I also like the way in which father's friend is sketched in simply as "My Dad's pal". We don't need to know too much about him – he is a pal of long-standing who, in a brilliantly-chosen phrase "dabbles in electricity". We also know that he seems to be a DIY-enthusiast, hence the disaster of the kitchen wall, and that he does the electrics for the drama company. It would have been easy to have started doing a pen portrait of "Dad's pal" during this piece, but by not doing so, Cath has allowed her story to keep to the main point – her Dad's DIY skills (or lack thereof).

This kind of writing is deceptively simple. Read it out loud and you will find it slipping easily off the tongue. This is a useful technique to develop. Make your work sound as conversational and as unforced as this and you will be doing very well indeed. This conversational tone also adds to the warmth of the piece, where even when the characters are obviously in conflict, they are still part of a family.

Bodies by Flo Wightman

The mounds of flesh all around me bounce and quiver in time to the throbbing beat.

Dripping with gold jewellery, semi naked, all are cleansed and polished for the occasion.

I had not wanted to come. Too old for this sort of thing. Have never seen so much naked flesh since skinny-dipping near St. Tropez when young, slim and lookable-at. This is not a Bacchanalian orgy but my first day at Over 60's

Aqua Fit. An orgy would only happen if men were allowed in our hallowed tub and they are not, though we live in hope. We are not allowed in the deep end until we are exhausted by the exercises, with any luck, once there, we will drown – it is a well known fact the class is oversubscribed.

We begin to line dance. Fine! Until our Leader (poolside), gives the order to move to the right. Some of us move to our right and some of us move to her right. We are no fools; we can dosey-doh with the best of them, no problem.

One of our main activities is adjusting straps. Everyone does it and it is totally unnecessary. If we all popped out together it would not matter. Unless of course we had a transvestite in our midst. This could not really happen, as, quite discreetly, we subject each other to minute scrutiny.

We would soon spot any bumps that should not be there.

Collectively we display all the ravages of time, bumps, bruises, spare tyres, saggy flesh, wrinkly flesh, FLESH. Melted down we would probably keep a furnace going for a week. We have all seen better days. Now there is too much of some of us, and not enough of others of us.

Next time I come I must look at the faces, they will probably be just as interesting as the bodies.

Often when we talk about writing our life stories, we talk about writing about events from our distant past. One of the real strengths of this piece is that we have the writer writing about herself in the present. It makes a change. It could also provide the springboard (if you'll pardon the swimming-pool pun) for some back story.

Another strength, of course, is the humour throughout the piece. Not just the self-deprecating humour about the flab and flesh, but also such jokes as "We are not allowed in the deep end until we are exhausted by the exercises, with any luck, once there, we will drown – it is a well-known fact the class is over-subscribed."

Again, Flo has done what several of the other writers have managed and that is to take something ordinary and mundane – in this case the Over 60's Aqua Fit Class – and turn it into something special. This is another example of how we don't have to be writing about an expedition by goat across sub-Saharan Africa in order to write good prose that others will want to read.

The Pleasures of the Tip by Audrey Paley

I was about ten years old when shown the delights of the council rubbish tip. Saturday was the best day, I was assured by my playmates, who dragged me towards the mounds of waste. These were mainly market-day sweepings from fruit and veg stalls and rich pickings were available.

"Come on, we've brought bags to put stuff in." Alan and David, brothers who lived across the road from me, urged me on by tugging my coat sleeves. The two youngest members skipped in front leading the way.

"Hurry up," they chorused, "or all the best things will have gone."

Clad in wellies and scruffy jumpers, we began scavenging. Sprouts, cabbages and carrots were stowed away – onions too if they weren't rotten. Mixed in with this assortment were pears, oranges and apples, some of the latter being eaten on the spot. Our plunder was gratefully received at home and turned into stews or fruit pies.

Best of all were the days when the drains were sucked clean. We loved it, despite the foul stench which didn't deter us a bit. The grey sludge was feverishly raked through with anything from garden trowels to old tablespoons and forks. In desperation, sometimes bare hands came into play.

"Found anything yet?" This came from Alan, the elder of the two brothers, who tried to rule the roost. "I wanna know what yer got so's we can share it."

Of course, nobody confessed to finding anything. Marbles were hastily wiped clean on stocking tops to reveal swirling bands of colour, before being quickly stuffed into pockets. There were also keys, buttons and odd coins, mostly coppers. Sometimes there was a glint of silver, making it difficult to keep quiet. Any whoops of delight brought the whole hunting party round that particular patch.

It was a sad day when we watched in disbelief as council workers erected a fence around the site and boards stating "Trespassers will be prosecuted" were hammered into the ground. The lucrative business was over.

Now doesn't this remind you of just how much fun it was to get really truly dirty as a child?

This is yet another example of taking an unlikely subject – in this case the council tip – and turning it into a wonderful piece of prose.

Throughout the piece, one is aware of the straightened circumstances in which people were living. The idea that they should be scavenging the waste of fruit and veg stalls is – by modern sensibilities – scandalous in the extreme. Yet at no point does Audrey make a huge case for how awful this poverty was. In fact, she does quite the reverse, turning the found delights of half-decent fruit into a treasure hunt.

Nor is there any reason for us to take pity on the protagonists of the story. They are enjoying themselves playing childhood games that just happen to involve scavenging the tip, the market-stall refuse and the drains. I love the way the clearing of the drains is described as "best of all".

There are several subtleties to this story-telling as well. We don't learn a great deal about Alan, save that as the eldest he feels himself to be their ringleader. We don't get huge physical descriptions of anyone – the children are "clad in wellies and scruffy jumpers". Similarly, whilst there is not a great deal of dialogue, what there is sticks to the point, most especially Alan's attempt to muscle in on any booty that might be better than his.

A Final Note

One of the great things about all these extracts is that they don't try to be too "writerly". It's a great mistake to think that writing is all about showing off your vocabulary, or proving your intelligence. Write in order to be understood.

All of them contain some human element to them. Yes, one of the reasons we should write about our lives is to capture the way places looked, but unless you put people into your landscape, it will make for dull writing. People want to read about people.

Now over to you

Well, that's the main part of the book over. There's just a few book lists and some other useful information to come.

I hope that from reading this little book, you now feel as though you can go about the task with relish.

Writing is fun It can be hard work. There may be days when you wonder why on earth you are doing it. There will be others when time flies and the muse smiles on you. Whether you rattle off pages at a time, or eke out words like drops of blood, one thing is certain. When you see the fruits of your labours in front of you, it gives you a real sense of achievement.

Your life story is important. It's just as important as that of Kings and Queens, Presidents and Prime Ministers or film stars and footballers. That is why you need to make sure that the way in which you write it is the best you can possibly manage.

So, good luck with your life story. If you're writing to amuse your family, I hope you raise a chuckle. If you're writing to make a lot of money, don't forget me when you're a multi-millionaire. Above all, enjoy doing it.

Appendix A – Further Reading

Autobiographies, Memoirs, Life Stories

These are some autobiographies I have enjoyed over the years. They're quite a mixed bag. I'd like to think it's because I read widely, but I suspect it's more likely to be because I'm a dilettante.

Boy - Tales of Childhood   Roald Dahl

Roald Dahl has such an easy style, he makes writing look simple. Although the book does feel like a diatribe against corporal punishment, the way Dahl captures the time and social milieu is excellent. Even if you don't like the book, the preface is worth using as a handy guide for your own writing.

If This is a Man   Primo Levi

Levi survived Hitler's death camps. Rarely can there have been anything on earth as hideously de-humanising as Nazi concentration camps. What I like about Levi's writing is that he doesn't sentimentalise. He tells his story directly. The compassion arises from the situations he describes and not from the over-wrought use of sentimental language.

Cider With Rosie   Laurie Lee

Laurie Lee was a poet, but his series of autobiographical books are what brought him fame. Cider with Rosie is the first and best of the series. I think it would be hard to emulate his poet's choice of words, but I love the way the book manages to progress chronologically, as well as being divided into themed chapters.

Portrait of the Artist as a Young Man   James Joyce

I actually studied this book at school, which should have put me off for life. It's not everyone's cup of tea, but it's interesting the way the language of the book develops as the child becomes older.

The Moon's A Balloon   David Niven

Often, celebrity autobiographies are a dismal hotchpotch of name-droppings. Niven's book is full of stories about the greats from Hollywood's Golden Age, but he manages to make it all sound like one great big adventure. I don't know how much of it is true, but I don't really care.

Fever Pitch   Nick Hornby

I'm not sure if you have to like football to like this book. What is interesting is the way in which Hornby, with wonderful self-irony, examines his obsession with Arsenal football club. It's very funny and a great example of how to use one main topic as an excuse for writing about all sorts of things – love, family, life in general.

Adolf Hitler – My Part in His Downfall   Spike Milligan

If you don't like Spike Milligan, you'll hate this book. I happen to think he was one of the funniest men who ever lived. Of course, a lot of the book is made up of gags and has to be taken with a pinch of salt, but I still think it's wonderful. It's a great antidote to all those "how I won the war single-handedly books" that appear every other year.

Post Office   Charles Bukowski

A very personal choice again. As with Milligan, if you don't like (or get) Bukowski's humour, you won't think much of this autobiographical novel. However, even if you don't like Bukowski's drinking, womanising and gambling (hey, a guy should have hobbies), then you might like the idea that he simply takes a cross-section of his life – his years working for the U.S. Post Office – and writes about that.

Experience   Martin Amis

OK, so Mart does go on about his dental adventures a little too much in this book, but it is fascinating to see his relationship with his father, Kingsley.

Oranges are not the Only Fruit   Jeanette Winterson

I'm not too keen on the little allegorical sections of the book, but Winterson's tales of her religious upbringing are witty, humorous and ultimately, sad.

Opening Up   Mike Atherton

Most sports stars would have got a ghost writer to do all the hard work for them. Mike Atherton didn't. If you don't like cricket, you probably won't enjoy this at all, but if you do, it makes a refreshing change from the usual rag-bag of clichés trotted out in most players' autobiographies.

The Kiss   Kathryn Harrison

A bizarre subject – the author's incestuous affaire with her estranged father – but beautifully written and far better than most confessional memoirs.

My Family and Other Animals   Gerald Durrell

It's perhaps a little dated now, but Durrell's tales of family life on Corfu has a cracking cast of eccentrics – and not just the Durrell family.

The Belljar   Sylvia Plath

Sylvia Plath is probably most famous for being the suicidal wife of Ted Hughes. She was a great poet in her own right and this is an autobiographical novel about her early adulthood that goes some way to explaining just how fragile a person she was.

Other Autobiographies That Are Worth A Look

Taken on Trust
Terry Waite
Portrait of the Artist as a Young Dog
Dylan Thomas
A Boy's Own Story
Edmund White
Empire of the Sun
J.G.Ballard
A Heartbreaking Work of Staggering Genius
Dave Eggers
The Adoption Papers
Jackie Kay
I Know Why the Caged Bird Sings
Maya Angelou
The Colour Purple
Alice Walker
Diana's Story
Deric Longden
Angela's Ashes
Frank McCourt
Tuppence To Cross The Mersey
Helen Forrester
Bad Blood
Lorna Sage

Reference Books

Everyone has their own preferred reference books I suggest that
a minimum requirement is something along these lines:

- A good-quality thesaurus
- A large single-volume English dictionary
- Whitaker's Almanac
- A good single volume encyclopaedia, e.g. Pears
- Brewer's Dictionary of Phrase and Fable

- Book of Quotations – ones that are arranged thematically are best
- "On this day" or an equivalent publication which gives details of anniversaries etc.
- Chronology of 20th Century

Handbooks

If you want to start selling your work, then you will find one of these two books essential reading. There's not much to choose between them. Both are published annually. I buy them alternate years:

The Writer's Handbook, edited by Barry Turner, published by Macmillan

Writers and Artists Yearbook, published by A & C Black

Books on Writing

If you get the writing bug and want to take your writing further, you might find you want to delve into other areas of writing. There are many books available on the subject.

Straightforward Publishing, the publishers of this book, publishes several books that may be of interest to you. Check out their website at www.straightforwardco.co.uk.

As writing books are so individual, it is probably worth testing them out at the library if you can before buying the ones you like best and will continue to refer to. I would recommend the following general books:

Stephen King, On Writing, Hodder & Stoughton, ISBN 0-340-76996-3

Julia Bell & Paul Magrs, The Creative Writing Coursebook, Macmillan, ISBN 0-333-78225-9

John Singleton, The Creative Writing Workbook, Palgrave, ISBN 0-333-79216-5

Dorothea Brande, Becoming a Writer, Macmillan, ISBN 0-333-34673-4

There are also dozens of specialist books on how to write plays, short stories, screenplays, feature articles, etc. If you get the writing bug, it's worth looking into them.

Writers' Magazines

I always think it's worthwhile trying out a few writers' magazines just to help you get into the right kind of frame of mind for writing.

There are several magazines available over the counter from the newsagent, but you might also like to try:

The New Writer
PO Box 60
Cranbrook
Kent
TN17 2ZR

The New Writer is a specialist writers' magazine that prints short stories that short-listed for the Ian St James award, as well as useful articles on how to get your work published. It also prints details of competitions, what's new, etc.

Appendix B – Courses for Writers

You should find details of local courses at your nearest library. University Continuing Education departments, the Adult and Community Learning sections of Education Authorities, the Workers' Educational Association and Further Education Colleges all run courses. Writing is now a very popular activity and you should find something to fit the bill. You might also find the following contacts useful.

ARCA – The Adult Residential Colleges Association

This is an association of specialist colleges running short residential courses for adults in England, Northern Ireland and Wales. Many of the colleges offer writing-related courses at different times throughout the year.

> The Secretary
> Adult Residential Colleges Association
> PO Box 31
> Washbrook
> Ipswich
> IP8 3HP
> website: www.aredu.org.uk

If you use the website, you can connect directly to colleges and trawl for courses. If you write to ARCA, they will send you a leaflet giving details of colleges throughout England and Wales.

Rydal Hall

Opposite William Wordsworth's house at Rydal Mount in the English Lake District, Rydal Hall is a stately home owned by the diocese of Carlisle. There is a resident Christian community here, although there are plenty of secular activities going on. They also now organise what they call "activity retreats", including some writing courses. It's a fabulous place to go and both recharge the batteries and get excited about your work. There are regular prayers, but there is no pressure at all on those who chose not to join in.

> Rydal Hall
> Ambleside
> Cumbria
> LA22 9LX
> Telephone 015394 32050
> website: www.rydalhall.org
> email bookings@rydalhall.org

Arvon Foundation

Arvon is a group of residential centres specialising in teaching creative writing. They have centres in Yorkshire, Inverness-shire, Shropshire and Devon. They have courses suitable for all levels of writer. Head Office Address:

> Arvon Foundation
> 42a, Buckingham Palace Road
> London
> SW1W 0RE
> website: www.arvonfoundation.org

Appendix C – Organisations for Writers

There are several professional organisations for writers. Some of them are for dramatists or writers of screenplays. If you become serious in your writing, you might want to join the Society of Authors. You have to fulfil certain criteria to become a member. However, they can send you details of membership

Society of Authors
84 Drayton Gardens
London
SW10 9SB

They also produce several booklets of interest to the writer.

Appraisal Services for Writers

There are several of these, you will find them listed in writers' annuals. However, you can obtain sensible advice at realistic prices from:

Real Writers
PO Box 170
Chesterfield
Derbyshire
S40 1FE

They offer a reading & appraisal service. They are inexpensive & can be very useful. Send them a SAE for more details.

NAWG – National Association of Writers' Groups,

If you would rather join a writers' group rather than a course, then NAWG maintains a list of groups throughout the country. These are not all the writers' groups and circles, but those affiliated to NAWG. Again your library should have details of other writers' groups.

NAWG The Arts Centre Biddick Lane
Washington Tyne & wear NE38 2AB
website: www.nawg.co.uk

www.straightforwardco.co.uk

All titles, listed below, in the Straightforward Guides Series can be purchased online, using credit card or other forms of payment by going to www.straightfowardco.co.uk A discount of 25% per title is offered with online purchases.

Law
A Straightforward Guide to:
Consumer Rights
Bankruptcy Insolvency and the Law
Employment Law
Private Tenants Rights
Family law
Small Claims in the County Court
Contract law
Intellectual Property and the law
Divorce and the law
Leaseholders Rights
The Process of Conveyancing
Knowing Your Rights and Using the Courts
Producing Your own Will
Housing Rights
The Bailiff the law and You
Probate and The Law
Company law
What to Expect When You Go to Court
Guide to Competition Law
Give me Your Money-Guide to Effective Debt Collection
Caring for a Disabled Child

General titles
Letting Property for Profit
Buying, Selling and Renting property
Buying a Home in England and France
Bookkeeping and Accounts for Small Business

Creative Writing
Freelance Writing
Writing Your own Life Story
Writing performance Poetry
Writing Romantic Fiction
Speech Writing

Teaching Your Child to Read and write
Teaching Your Child to Swim
Raising a Child-The Early Years

Creating a Successful Commercial Website
The Straightforward Business Plan
The Straightforward C.V.
Successful Public Speaking

Handling Bereavement
Play the Game-A Compendium of Rules
Individual and Personal Finance
Understanding Mental Illness
The Two Minute Message
Guide to Self Defence
Buying a Used Car
Tiling for Beginners

Go to:

www.straightforwardco.co.uk